THE PENGUIN POETS

D 44

COLLECTED VERSE

HILAIRE BELLOC

HILAIRE BELLOC

COLLECTED VERSE

WITH AN INTRODUCTION BY

RONALD KNOX

PENGUIN BOOKS

Penguin Books Ltd, Harmondsworth, Middlesex
AUSTRALIA: Penguin Books Pty Ltd, 762 Whitehorse Road,
Mitcham, Victoria

—

Verses first published by Duckworth 1910
Sonnets and Verse first published 1923
New edition, with additional Poems, 1954
Published in the Penguin Poets 1958.

Made and printed in Great Britain
by Hazell Watson & Viney Ltd
Aylesbury and Slough

Contents

Sonnets of the Twelve Months

2. LYRICAL, DIDACTIC AND GROTESQUE

3. SONGS

4. BALLADES

5. EPIGRAMS   153

6. LONGER POEMS

The poems, 'Dirge', 'Duncton Hill', 'A Sussex Drinking Song' and 'My Own Country' are taken from *The Four Men* and included here by kind permission of the publishers of that volume, Thomas Nelson & Sons.

Introduction

Will the fame of Belloc represent him as a writer of verse, or as a writer of prose?

Long ago, at school, I competed for a poetry prize in which Arthur Benson was the examiner. He said to me, 'Go on writing poems; you will find it helps you to write prose.' The advice came from a suspect source; many people would have said that Arthur Benson had missed his vocation. But what do they think of themselves, these people who write poetry with one hand and prose with the other? And what ought we to think of them? The list, in our literature, is a surprisingly long one; you can name (at various levels of achievement) Donne, Milton, Dryden, Addison, Southey, Coleridge, Macaulay, Landor, Newman, Matthew Arnold, Stevenson, Mr Walter de la Mare, Mr Siegfried Sassoon; nor, evidently, is such a list complete. Does a man who possesses this gift of ambidexterity think of himself as a poet who occasionally condescends to prose? Or as a prose-writer who sometimes dabbles in verse? And which medium, in either case, best betrays the true man?

The subject of fame bothered Belloc; he has written of it, and in those later days, when his mind was apt to chew the cud of earlier meditations, it recurred in his talk continually. What was this curious illusion which the human mind can neither analyse nor renounce? I think if he had been offered the choice whether he would rather be remembered by his prose or by his verse, he would have chosen the latter. He used to say that of all his books only four really satisfied him – I am not sure which, but *Belinda* would certainly have been named among them. It was his affectation to talk, sometimes, as if he wrote only for money; poverty and the publishers never allowed him to 'linger in his rightful garden' – that of verse.

Verse he called it, not out of modesty, I think, but because he was old-fashioned enough to think of poetry as something which must be polished and repolished until it was perfect in form. This does him no good with the moderns; our critics, in every kind of art, will only let us admire what is flung at us as a smudge, supposedly representing some impression in the artist's mind, all the better for being shapeless. To smell of the midnight oil damns you. Of such contemporary movements Belloc showed little consciousness, although *The Missing Masterpiece* gives us a hint of what he thought about them. His, in any case, was the classical tradition, deeply rooted in him as in Maurice Baring, though in either case it was difficult to see whence it had sprung. He always talked as if they had taught him precious little Latin and Greek at the Oratory, but his letters written at the time make us hesitate to accept his estimate. I have a copy of *Caliban* in which he inscribed two very mournful lines from the Iliad, with four wrong (but quite plausible) accents to show that he did not copy the quotation out of a book. He belonged to that period, that culture, in which a receptive mind refreshed itself, almost unconsciously, at the spring of the Classics.

The same influence penetrated into his style, derivatively, through his admiration of French poetry, and especially that of the Augustan period. When he wanted an instance of superlatively good literature, he referred you to *Le Misanthrope*. Of our own poets I think his favourite, in spite of a profound divergence of temperament, was Milton. In architecture he proclaimed, tirelessly, the Gothic; in literature, it seems to me, all his feeling was for the baroque, its marble simplicity, its dignified restraint. If you want to place him among English poets, you must not put him side by side with his contemporaries, or even with the Victorians. He belongs to the classical period which began with Milton, and ended (for most of us) with Gray.

He belongs to the classical period in his mastery of cadence. By which I mean, not a mere manipulation of sounds, with a musical effect, quite divorced from the sense of what you are saying, and sometimes compelling you to say it unconvincingly – you get it *ad nauseam* in Swinburne. I mean that perfect marriage of sound and sense which now and again, especially in the rounding-off of a poem, creates a kind of stillness in the mind. Such lines, I mean, as:

> They also serve, who only stand and wait,

or:

> And universal darkness buries all.

It is not unknown, to be sure, in recent poetry – Housman knew the magic of it – but Belloc is continually achieving it. In such lines, I mean, as:

> . . . and having seen that stone
> (Which was your image), ride more slowly on,

or:

> And her lips virginal,
> Her virginal white feet,

or (with a devastatingly conversational effect):

On with my coat and out into the night.

There may be those who are unmoved by such effects; who think them artificial, thought up. Certainly the moderns have no use for them. I only note that they were dear to the Augustans, and to Belloc.

He belongs to the classical period in the strong intellectual background of his poetry. I do not mean that he set out to mystify us, as the metaphysical poets did, or Browning. I mean that he was nearly always trying to *say* something; he would not be content merely to record an impression. And this again distinguishes him from the moderns, though not so certainly from the Victorians. But it is more noticeably true of the older poets; there was brain in what they wrote. Consider, for instance, that a competent schoolboy could write you an intelligible *précis* of Gray's Elegy; all the magic and the music would be gone, but you would learn what the poem was about. But a schoolboy's *précis* which began 'The author declares his intention of going to Innisfree and building nine bean-rows there' would leave no impression on the mind at all. There is brain in the verses Belloc wrote, even (very noticeably) in his Nonsense Verses, where you might have expected him to leave it behind. He must build; he could not be merely receptive.

He belongs to the classical period because he was, by instinct and by taste, a satirist. It is a curious fact that among the English poets who were his predecessors (unless you regard *Hudibras* as poetry, or Byron as satire) only two were professional satirists, Dryden and Pope. Both used the heroic couplet, with its bite, its detachment, its finality. And in this sort Belloc was – or could have been – a master. This does not appear only in his epigrams, although it is most noticeable in his epigrams. I doubt if the possibilities of the heroic couplet have ever been exploited more fully than in the lines:

The accurséd power which stands on Privilege
(And goes with women, and champagne, and bridge)
Broke – and democracy resumed her reign;
(Which goes with bridge, and women, and champagne).

But he used it at length in *To Dives*, and returned to it for his *Heroic Poem in Praise of Wine*. You may call it *pastiche*, if you will, when he writes a perfect couplet like:

15

> The dank despisers of the Vine arise
> To watch grey dawns, and mourn indifferent skies;

but to be capable of such *pastiche* is to be capable of something beyond mere imitation. One who could so master the secret of Dryden and Pope could, given the opportunity, have written as they did.

'Given the opportunity' – the phrase recalls us to our original question, 'Will Belloc be remembered as a poet, or as a prose-writer?' Probably as a prose-writer, for no better reason than that his verse output was, by comparison, so small. Ordinarily, the reading public demands a certain level of industry before it will admit a poet to the privileges of immortality; Gray is the shining exception who proves the rule. It is with Belloc as with Johnson; his prose so notably exceeds his verse in mere volume that he is likely to be remembered as a prose-writer who occasionally tried his hand at verse. In his own estimation he was a poet *manqué*; Mr Sheed, who questioned him directly on the subject, ascertained that this was the meaning of his phrase,

> Nor ever in my rightful garden lingered;

and the context of the line (it occurs at the end of *Stanzas written on Battersea Bridge*) shows that he felt it as a grievance. England (and perhaps at the back of his mind he meant Oxford) had refused him something: the leisure to write what he would, as he would. If (*per impossibile*) he had been content to get a Civil Service job on going down from Balliol, he might have dedicated to the Muses those long evenings during which the Inland Revenue had no use for him. As it was, his time and talents were (he felt) being prostituted to the claims of editor and publisher who wanted copy and were content with his second best.

He was, as I have indicated, a man who could not be satisfied with the verse he had written until it had been polished and repolished, recast perhaps, in its perfect form. In his early days, he was no doubt resigned to the experience of not getting things finished, and put it down to his own indolence. You get the echo of such feelings at the beginning of the *Path to Rome:* 'What about that little lyric on Winchelsea that you thought of writing six years ago? Why are the lines still in your head and not on paper? Because you can't begin. However, never mind, you can't help it; it's your one great flaw, and it's fatal.' When, in middle life, he found that he was still lecturing, still working at biographies which did not really interest him, he felt a grievance about not being allowed to get on with his poetry. The *Heroic Poem in Praise of Wine* was finished late and with difficulty; the *Ode to the West Wind*, of which some fragments were already in his mind, never got finished at all. He had produced a respectable number of sonnets, but he was not sure of them; the number of them varies from edition to edition, as if his own judgement had become more exacting. For the rest, there was more variety than bulk in his output, unless you included the Nonsense Verse. If staying-power enters into the definition of a poet, if he must needs put up a brass plate that says 'Poet' at his front door, Belloc is not among the poets. It is even doubtful whether, on those terms, he would have wished to be. It is impossible to doubt that the different characters in *The Four Men* are in a sense Belloc's own selves, and for the Poet he has an evident though a kindly contempt.

There is another consideration which may, I think, prejudice Belloc's chances of being ranked among the immortals. Rightly or wrongly, we think of each poet as having a vein or genius of his own; his moods may alter, his mannerisms may grow upon him, but there is something in his outlook upon life which remains constant and recognizable. Quite apart from any question of metre or diction, we should give no marks at all to a schoolboy who guessed – that the *Scholar Gipsy* was by Swinburne, or *Abt Vogler* by Housman. Belloc, when he sat down to write poetry, had a genius, a vein of his own, like the rest of them. (Chesterton had a feeling for Battersea, but he would not have written the *Stanzas on Battersea Bridge*.) But a great deal of what Belloc wrote in verse was written without sitting down; scribbled on the back of an envelope or extemporized when there were songs being sung. And so inspired was he, even in his most irresponsible moments, that you cannot write off these lesser effusions of his, like the Juvenilia of Tennyson, or the tameness of Keats in his lighter moods. He will always be judged, to a great extent, by fugitive pieces which, in a collected edition of his own works, he would have polished or suppressed.

The truth is he was too many-sided a man to put only a part of himself into anything he wrote. His gift was for satire; but it is the business of your satirist to be quite inhuman, never to drop the mask of scorn which divides him from his readers. Belloc would drop the mask without warning. The last few pages of *Emmanuel Burden* are as good as anything in English prose, but they are innocent of satire. So with the *Ballade of Illegal Ornaments*, which begins as a light-hearted commentary on the ecclesiastical happenings of the day, and ends up, as we know:

17

> Prince Jesus, in mine agony,
>   Permit me, broken and defiled,
> Through blurred and glazing eyes to see
>   A Female Figure with a Child.

The *volte-face* is enormously effective, but it disconcerts the conscientious editor who is determined to label the poems and divide them up into sections according to the mood in which they were written. Sometimes, of course, the *volte-face* will be the other way round:

> Prince, on their iron thrones they sit,
>   Impassible to our despair,
> The dreadful Guardians of the Pit: –
>   And Mrs Roebeck will be there.

What is the fellow about? Is he to be taken seriously, or with a grain of salt? Is he to be classed with Rabelais, or with George Herbert? Criticism does not love the unpredictable.

Actually, it may be doubted whether Belloc was not too much of a humorist to be a straight satirist, and *vice versa*. The satirist, for the sake of contrast, ought to take himself seriously; in Belloc, there was a streak of humility which let down the average – he could laugh at himself. I still picture him, one New Year's eve, reading aloud to his family my brother's parody of his own poem on Sussex, and shouting with laughter. You are not prepared for his sudden condescensions to the ludicrous – as when you find, among his published sonnets, one which begins,

> Would that I had £300,000.

Contrariwise, as I have suggested above, the trouble about his Nonsense Verses is that they are so full of good sense. When Lear writes nonsense, or Lewis Carroll, you find only a jingle of sounds, which has nothing in common with serious poetry except rhyme and metre. When Belloc sat down to the same task, the imp of satire was for ever perched on his shoulder; and there is a whole world of social history in such lines as:

> The people in between
>   Looked underdone and harassed,
> And commonplace and mean,
>   And horribly embarrassed.

I read *The Modern Traveller* as a boy, and loved it; so, too, as a boy, I read *Gulliver's Travels*, and loved them; but in the one case as the other, I was never really conscious of what it was all about.

You cannot divide up Belloc's poetry, as you can divide up Hood's, into Serious and Comic; the two qualifications overlap and interlock; in letters, as in life, the severity of his lips is pulled downwards, all of a sudden, into a smile.

To make him all the more unclassifiable, Belloc was a songwriter. This is a trick quite distinct from poetry; the Elizabethans had it, but it is rare among the moderns. Belloc was one of those people who, perhaps to work off their high spirits, perhaps to conceal their low spirits, will for ever be bursting into song. I remember his driving me from Arundel to King's Land singing at the wheel all the way. And when his repertoire failed, he would make up songs of his own, sometimes with tunes of his own, a feat hardly imaginable in Pope, say, or Wordsworth. If every other record of him should perish, it is to be hoped that posterity will be able to hear, on a gramophone record, *Ha'nacker Mill* as it was sung by its own author and composer. That last haunting line, 'Never a ploughman. Never a one' will perpetuate his genius, and his sadness. But how to place him? How to rank *Ha'nacker Mill* among the other classics?

Nullum fere scribendi genus non tetigit, nullum quod tetigit non ornavit; is it only Goldsmith that deserves the epitaph? And is there no immortality for the versatile?

1956   RONALD KNOX

I
SONNETS

Sonnets

I

Lift up your hearts in Gumber, laugh the Weald
And you my mother the Valley of Arun sing.
Here am I homeward from my wandering,
Here am I homeward and my heart is healed.
You my companions whom the World has tired
Come out to greet me. I have found a face
More beautiful than Gardens; more desired
Than boys in exile love their native place.

Lift up your hearts in Gumber, laugh the Weald
And you most ancient Valley of Arun sing.
Here am I homeward from my wandering,
Here am I homeward and my heart is healed.
If I was thirsty, I have heard a spring.
If I was dusty, I have found a field.

II

I was like one that keeps the deck by night
    Bearing the tiller up against his breast;
I was like one whose soul is centred quite
    In holding course although so hardly prest,
And veers with veering shock now left now right,
    And strains his foothold still and still makes play
Of bending beams until the sacred light
    Shows him high lands and heralds up the day.

But now such busy work of battle past
I am like one whose barque at bar at last
Comes hardly heeling down the adventurous breeze;
And entering calmer seas,
I am like one that brings his merchandise
    To Californian skies.

III

Whatever moisture nourishes the Rose,
The Rose of the World in laughter's garden-bed
Where Souls of men on faith secure are fed
And spirits immortal keep their pleasure-close.
Whatever moisture nourishes the Rose,
The burning Rose of the World, for me the same
Today for me the spring without a name
Content or Grace or Laughter overflows.

This is that water from the Fount of Gold
Water of Youth and washer out of cares
Which Raymond of Saragossa sought of old
And finding in the mountain, unawares,
Returned to hear an ancient story told
To Bramimond, his love, beside the marble stairs.

IV

Youth gave you to me, but I'll not believe
That Youth will, taking his quick self, take you.
Youth's all our Truth: he cannot so deceive.
He has our graces, not our ownselves too.
He still compares with time when he'll be spent,
By human doom enhancing what we are;
Enriches us with rare experiment,
Lends arms to leaguered Age in Time's rough war.

Look! This Youth in us is an Old Man taking
A Boy to make him wiser than his days.
So is our old Youth our young Age's making:
So rich in time our final debt he pays.
　　Then with your quite young arms do you me hold
　　And I will still be young when all the World's grown old.

V

Mortality is but the Stuff you wear
To show the better on the imperfect sight.
Your home is surely with the changeless light
Of which you are the daughter and the heir.
For as you pass, the natural life of things
Proclaims the Resurrection: as you pass
Remembered summer shines across the grass
And somewhat in me of the immortal sings.

You were not made for memory, you are not
Youth's accident I think but heavenly more;
Moulding to meaning slips my pen's poor blot
And opening wide that long forbidden door
　　Where stands the Mother of God, your exemplar.
　　How beautiful, how beautiful you are!

VI

Not for the luckless buds our roots may bear
　　Now all in bloom, now seared and cankered lying
Will I entreat you, lest they should compare
　　Foredoomed humanity with the fall of flowers.
Hold thou with me the chaste communion rare
　　And touch with life this mortal case of ours;
　　You're lifted up beyond the power of dying:
I die, as bounded things die everywhere.

　　You're voiced companionship, I'm silence lonely;
You're stuff, I'm void; you're living, I'm decay.
　　I fall, I think, to night and ending only;
You rise, I know, through still advancing day.
　　And knowing living gift were life for me
　　In narrow room of rhyme I fixed it certainly.

That which is one they shear and make it twain
Who would Love's light and dark discriminate:
His pleasure is one essence with his pain,
Even his desire twin brother to his hate.
With him the foiled attempt is half achieving;
And being mastered, to be armed a lord;
And doubting every chance is still believing;
And losing all one's own is all reward.

I am acquainted with misfortune's fortune,
And better than herself her dowry know:
For she that is my fortune and misfortune,
Making me hapless, makes me happier so:
In which conceit, as older men may prove,
Lies manifest the very core of Love.

Shall any man for whose strong love another
    Has thrown away his wealth and name in one,
Shall he turn mocker of a more than brother
    To slight his need when his adventure's done?
Or shall a breedless boy whose mother won him
    In great men's great concerns his little place
Turn when his farthing honours come upon him
    To mock her yeoman air and conscious grace?

Then mock me as you do my narrow scope,
    For you it was put out this light of mine:
Wrongfully wrecked my new adventured hope,
    Wasted my wordy wealth, spilt my rich wine,
Made my square ship within a league of shore
    Alas! to be entombed in seas and seen no more.

They that have taken wages of things done
When sense abused has blocked the doors of sense,
They that have lost their heritage of the sun,
Their laughter and their holy innocence;
They turn them now to this thing, now to t'other,
For anchor hold against swift-eddying time,
Some to that square of earth which was their mother,
And some to noisy fame, and some to rhyme.

But I to that far morning where you stood
In fullness of the body, with your hands
Reposing on your walls, before your lands,
And all, together, making one great good:
    Then did I cry 'For this my birth was meant.
    These are my use, and this my sacrament!'

X

Beauty that Parent is to deathless Rhyme
Was Manhood's maker: you shall bear a Son,
Till Daughters linked adown admiring time
Fulfil the mother, handing Beauty on.
You shall by breeding make Life answer yet,
In Time's despite, Time's jeer that men go void;
Your stamp of heaven shall be more largely set
Than my one joy, ten thousand times enjoyed.

The glories of our state and its achievement,
Which wait their passing, shall not pass away.
I will extend our term beyond bereavement,
And launch our date into a dateless day.
    For you shall make recórd, and when that's sealed
    In Beauty made immortal, all is healed.

What are the names for Beauty? Who shall praise
God's pledge he can fulfil His creatures' eyes?
Or what strong words of what creative phrase
Determine Beauty's title in the skies?
But I will call you Beauty Personate,
Ambassadorial Beauty, and again
Beauty triumphant, Beauty in the Gate,
Beauty salvation of the souls of men.

For Beauty was not Beauty till you came
And now shall Beauty mean the sign you are;
A Beacon burnt above the Dawn, a flame
Like holy Lucifer the Morning Star,
    Who latest hangs in Heaven and is the gem
    On all the widowed Night's expectant Diadem.

Love wooing Honour, Honour's love did win
And had his pleasure all a summer's day.
Not understanding how the dooms begin,
Love wooing Honour, wooed her life away.
Then wandered he a full five years unrest
Until, one night, this Honour that had died
Came as he slept, in youth grown glorified
And smiling like the Saints whom God has blest.

But when he saw her on the clear night shine
Serene with more than mortal light upon her,
The boy that careless was of things divine,
Small Love, turned penitent to worship Honour.
    So Love can conquer Honour: when that's past
    Dead Honour risen outdoes Love at last.

Your life is like a little winter's day
Whose sad sun rises late to set too soon;
You have just come – why will you go away,
Making an evening of what should be noon?
Your life is like a little flute complaining
A long way off, beyond the willow trees:
A long way off, and nothing left remaining
But memory of a music on the breeze.

Your life is like a pitiful leave-taking
Wept in a dream before a man's awaking,
A Call with only shadows to attend:
A Benediction whispered and belated
Which has no fruit beyond a consecrated,
A consecrated silence at the end.

XIV

Now shall the certain purpose of my soul
By blind and empty things controlléd be,
And mine audacious course to that far goal
Fall short, confessing mere mortality.
Limbs shall have movement and ignore their living,
Brain wit, that he his quickness may deny.
My promised hope forswears in act of giving,
Time eats me up and makes my words a lie.

And mine unbounded dream has found a bar,
And I must worst deceit of best things bear.
Now dawn's but daybreak, seas but waters are,
Night darkness only, all wide heaven just air:
   And you to whom these fourteen lines I tell,
   My beauty, my desire: but not my love as well.

Because my faltering feet may fail to dare
The first descendant of the steps of Hell,
Give me the Word in time that triumphs there.
I too must pass into the misty hollow
Where all our living laughter stops: and hark!
The tiny stuffless voices of the dark
Have called me, called me, till I needs must follow:
Give me the Word and I'll attempt it well.

Say it's the little winking of an eye
Which in that issue is uncurtained quite;
A little sleep that helps a moment by
Between the thin dawn and the large daylight.
   Ah! tell me more than yet was hoped of men;
   Swear that's true now, and I'll believe it then.

When you to Acheron's ugly water come
Where darkness is and formless mourners brood,
And down the shelves of that distasteful flood
Survey the human rank in order dumb:
When the pale dead go forward, tortured more
By nothingness and longing than by fire,
Which bear their hands in suppliance with desire,
With stretched desire for the ulterior shore:

Then go before them like a royal ghost
And tread like Egypt or like Carthage crowned;
Because in your Mortality the most
Of all we may inherit has been found —
   Children for memory: the Faith for pride:
   Good land to leave: and young Love satisfied.

We will not whisper, we have found the place
Of silence and the endless halls of sleep:
And that which breathes alone throughout the deep,
The end and the beginning: and the face
Between the level brows of whose blind eyes
Lie plenary contentment, full surcease
Of violence, and the passionless long peace
Wherein we lose our human lullabies.

Look up and tell the immeasurable height
Between the vault of the world and your dear head;
That's death, my little sister, and the night
Which was our Mother beckons us to bed,
    Where large oblivion in her house is laid
    For us tired children, now our games are played.

XVIII

I went to sleep at Dawn in Tuscany
Beneath a Rock and dreamt a morning dream.
I thought I stood by that baptismal stream
Whereon the bounds of our redemption lie.
And there, beyond, a radiance rose to take
My soul at passing, in which light your eyes
So filled me I was drunk with Paradise.
Then the day broadened, but I did not wake.

Here's the last edge of my long parchment furled
And all was writ that you might read it so.
This sleep I swear shall last the length of day;
Not noise, not chance, shall drive this dream away:
Not time, not treachery, not good fortune – no,
Not all the weight of all the wears of the world.

Almighty God, whose justice like a sun
Shall coruscate along the floors of Heaven,
Raising what's low, perfecting what's undone,
Breaking the proud and making odd things even.
The poor of Jesus Christ along the street,
In your rain sodden, in your snows unshod,
They have nor hearth, nor sword, nor human meat,
Nor even the bread of men: Almighty God.

The poor of Jesus Christ whom no man hears
Have waited on your vengeance much too long.
Wipe out not tears but blood: our eyes bleed tears.
Come smite our damnéd sophistries so strong
That thy rude hammer battering this rude wrong
Ring down the abyss of twice ten thousand years.

Mother of all my cities, once there lay
　　About your weedy wharves an orient shower
　　Of spice and languorous silk and all the dower
That Ocean gave you on his bridal day.
And now the youth and age have passed away
　　And all the sail superb and all the power;
　　Your time's a time of memory like that hour
Just after sunset, wonderful and grey.

Too tired to rise and much too sad to weep,
　　With strong arm nerveless on a nerveless knee,
Still to your slumbering ears the spousal deep
　　Murmurs his thoughts of eld eternally;
But your soul wakes not from its holy sleep
Dreaming of dead delights beside a tideless sea.

O my companion, O my sister Sleep.
The valley is all before us, bear me on.
High through the heaven of evening, hardly gone,
Beyond the harbour lights, beyond the steep,
Beyond the land and its lost benison
To where, majestic on the darkening deep,
The night comes forward from Mount Aurion.
O my companion, O my sister Sleep.

Above the surf-line, into the night-breeze;
Eastward above the ever-whispering seas;
Through the warm airs with no more watch to keep.
My day's run out and all its dooms are graven.
O dear forerunner of Death and promise of Haven.
O my companion, O my sister Sleep.

XXII

Are you the end, Despair, or the poor least
    Of them that cast great shadows and are lies?
    That dread the simple and destroy the wise,
Fail at the tomb and triumph at the feast?
You were not found on Olivet, dull beast,
    Nor in Thebaid, when the night's agonies
    Dissolved to glory on the effulgent east
And Jesus Christ was in the morning skies.

You did not curb the indomitable crest
    Of Tzerna-Gora, when the Falcon-bred
        Screamed over the Adriatic, and their Lord
Went riding out, much angrier than the rest,
    To summon at ban the living and the dead
        And break the Mahommedan with the repeated sword.

XXIII

But oh! not Lovely Helen, nor the pride
Of that most ancient Ilium matched with doom.
Men murdered Priam in his royal room
And Troy was burned with fire and Hector died.
For even Hector's dreadful day was more
Than all his breathing courage dared defend;
The armoured light and bulwark of the war
Trailed his great story to the accustomed end.

He was the city's buttress, Priam's Son,
The Soldier, born in bivouac – praises great
And horns in double front of battle won.
Yet down he went: when unremembering fate
Felled him at last with all his armour on.
Hector: the horseman: in the Scaean Gate.

XXIV

The world's a stage. The light is in one's eyes.
The Auditorium is extremely dark.
The more dishonest get the larger rise;
The more offensive make the greater mark.
The women on it prosper by their shape,
Some few by their vivacity. The men,
By tailoring in breeches and in cape.
The world's a stage – I say it once again.

The scenery is very much the best
Of what the wretched drama has to show,
Also the prompter happens to be dumb.
We drink behind the scenes and pass a jest
On all our folly; then, before we go
Loud cries for 'Author' . . . but he doesn't come.

The world's a stage – and I'm the Super man,
And no one seems responsible for salary.
I roar my part as loudly as I can
And all I mouth I mouth it to the gallery.
I haven't got another rhyme in 'alery';
It would have made a better job, no doubt,
If I had left attempt at Rhyming out,
Like Alfred Tennyson adapting Malory.

The world's a stage, the company of which
Has very little talent and less reading:
But many a waddling heathen painted bitch
And many a standing cad of gutter breeding.
    We sweat to learn our book: for all our pains
    We pass. The Chucker-out alone remains.

The world's a stage. The trifling entrance fee
Is paid (by proxy) to the registrar.
The Orchestra is very loud and free
But plays no music in particular.
They do not print a programme, that I know.
The cast is large. There isn't any plot.
The acting of the piece is far below
The very worst of modernistic rot.

The only part about it I enjoy
Is what was called in English the Foyay.
There will I stand apart awhile and toy
With thought, and set my cigarette alight;
And then – without returning to the play –
On with my coat and out into the night.

XXVII

They that have been beside us all the day
  Rise up; for they are summoned to the gate.
Nor turn the head but take a downward way;
  Depart, and leave their households desolate.
But you shall not depart, although you leave
  My house for conversation with your peers.
Your admirable Ghost shall not receive
  Mere recollected vows and secret tears.

But on that brink of Heaven where lingering stand
  The still-remembrant spirits hearkening down,
Go, tower among them all, to hear the land,
  To hear the land alive with your renown.
    Nor strength, nor peace, nor laughter could I give,
    But this great wages: after death, to live.

XXVIII

Of meadows drowsy with Trinacrian bees,
Of shapes that moved a rising mist among —
Persephone between the Cypress trees —
Of lengthier shades along the woodland flung,
Of calm upon the hardly whispering seas,
Of cloud that to the distant island clung —
He made of emerald evening and of these
A holier song than ever yet was sung.

But silence and the single-thoughted night,
Hearing such music took him for their own
To that long land, where, men forgotten quite,
Harpless he errs by Lethe stream alone.
He never more will know that wind-flower's white —
He never more shall hear uneasy autumn moan.

Would that I had £300,000
　Invested in some strong security;
A Midland Country House with formal grounds,
　A Town House, and a House beside the sea,
And one in Spain, and one in Normandy,
　And Friends innumerable at my call
And youth serene – and underneath it all
　One steadfast, passionate flame to nurture me.

Then would I chuck for good my stinking trade
　Of writing tosh at 1s. 6d. a quire!
And soar like young Bellerophon arrayed
　High to the filmy Heavens of my desire. . . .
　　But that's all over. Here's the world again.
　　Bring me the Blotter. Fill the fountain-pen.

XXX

Do not believe when lovely lips report
That I lost anchor in rough seas of jest,
Or turned, in false confusion manifest,
To pleading folly in high beauty's court;
Or said of that you do (which in the doing
You maim yourself) what things I could not say,
For dread of unassuaged remorse ensuing
On one light word which haunts us all our way.

That I grow sour, who only lack delight;
That I descend to sneer, who only grieve:
That from my depth I should contemn your height;
That with my blame my mockery you receive;
Huntress and splendour of the woodland night,
Diana of this world, do not believe.

Believing Truth is staring at the sun
Which but destroys the power that could perceive.
So naught of our poor selves can be at one
With burning Truth, nor utterly believe.
For we that mortal are, to our derision,
Must soften certitude with that which seems,
And slake in dull repose a blinding vision,
Buy light with dark, and sleep for sake of dreams.

Mistrust, I do require you, all you trust,
And mock continuance of a steadfast mood,
And taste in all your joys their coming dust,
And call the endless flight of goodness, good.
Save in one article – Doubt earth and sea,
Doubt all that stands and is, but doubt not me.

XXXII

Believe too little and go down despairing;
Believe too much and lose it at the end.
Believe in none and die of over-caring;
Believe in all and die without a friend.
Believe in what's to come and still go grieving;
Believe in what's gone by and find it fades.
Believe in not insisting on believing
For all believing's but a dance of shades.

But oh! believe in me! I ask no more –
And you no more of sustenance shall need;
For that's a food ambrosial which can feed
The soul with sendings from th'Elysian shore,
As though contents eternal breathed abroad.
But don't believe in Phémé; she's a fraud.

Because I find foreknowledge in my soul
Of your true sisterhood with heavenly things,
And see from tardier years that further goal
Youth hides from you with its imaginings,
And witness am to your inheritance
And see beneath the passing of your grace
Un-passing calms, and a perfected face
Immutable; prefigured in a glance –

Therefore did I and therefore now complain
That you're profaned, and daily do renew
To make your own resplendent beauty vain
Through mimic beauty of what's likest you.
This was my sentence. This was all my say;
Mourning such light beclouded in a play.

XXXIV

Oh! do not play me music any more,
   Lest in us mortal some not mortal spell
   Should stir strange hopes, and leave a tale to tell
Of two beloved whom holy music bore,
   Through whispering night and doubt's uncertain seas,
To drift at length along a dawnless shore,
   The last sad goal of human harmonies.
Look! do not play me music any more.

You are my music and my mistress both,
   Why, then, let music play the master here?
Make silent melody, Melodie. I am loath
   To find that music, large in my soul's ear,
Should stop my fancy, hold my heart in prize,
And make me dreamer more than dreams are wise.

XXXV

As one who hath sent forth on a bold emprise
Into some distant land his Argosies
Watches in dread the fitful changing breeze,
And as now soft, now rude, its voices rise,
So hopes, so fears, for his far merchandise,
(Though that in other climes have other seas),
I, anxious too that this my plea should please,
Gaze still upon the mystery of your eyes;
The which, now laughing, now provoking sorrow,
Most like a fitful breeze have seemed to me;
But roofy night can breed an open morrow,
And these rough winds give earnest presently
Of days when, heeling down the waves, shall come
All my dear fleet and all my risked adventures Home.

XXXVI

(FOR EASTER SUNDAY)

Though Man made wine, I think God made it too;
God, making all things, made Man make good wine.
He taught him how the little tendrils twine
About the stakes of labour close and true.
Then next, with intimate prophetic laughter,
He taught the Man, in His own image blest,
To pluck and waggon and to – all the rest!
To tread the grape and work his vintage after.

So did God make us, making good wine's makers;
So did he order us to rule the field.
And now by God are we not only bakers
But vintners also, sacraments to yield;
Yet most of all strong lovers. Praised be God!
Who taught us how the wine-press should be trod.

Sonnets of the Twelve Months

JANUARY

It freezes: all across a soundless sky
The birds go home. The governing dark's begun.
The steadfast dark that waits not for a sun;
The ultimate dark wherein the race shall die.
Death with his evil finger to his lip
Leers in at human windows, turning spy
To learn the country where his rule shall lie
When he assumes perpetual generalship.

The undefeated enemy, the chill
That shall benumb the voiceful earth at last,
Is master of our moment, and has bound
The viewless wind itself. There is no sound.
It freezes. Every friendly stream is fast.
It freezes, and the graven twigs are still.

FEBRUARY

The Winter Moon has such a quiet car
That all the winter nights are dumb with rest.
She drives the gradual dark with drooping crest
And dreams go wandering from her drowsy star.
Because the nights are silent, do not wake.
But there shall tremble through the general earth,
And over you, a quickening and a birth.
The Sun is near the hill-tops for your sake.

The latest born of all the days shall creep
To kiss the tender eyelids of the year;
And you shall wake, grown young with perfect sleep,
And smile at the new world and make it dear
    With living murmurs more than dreams are deep;
    Silence is dead, my dawn, the morning's here.

The north-east wind has come from Norroway,
  Roaring he came above the white waves' tips!
  The foam of the loud sea was on his lips,
And all his hair was salt with falling spray.
Over the keen light of northern day
  He cast his snow cloud's terrible eclipse;
  Beyond our banks he suddenly struck the ships,
And left them labouring on his landward way.

The certain course that to his strength belongs
Drives him with gathering purpose and control
  Until across Vendean flats he sees
  Ocean, the eldest of his enemies.
Then wheels he for him, glorying in his goal,
And gives him challenge, bellowing battle-songs.

APRIL

The stranger warmth of the young sun obeying,
  Look! little heads of green begin to grow,
  And hidden flowers have dared their tops to show
Where late such droughty dusts were rudely playing.
It's not the month, but all the world's a-maying!
  Come then with me, I'll take you, for I know
  Where the first hedgethorns and white windflowers blow:
We two alone, that goes without the saying.

The month has treacherous clouds and moves in fears.
  This April shames the month itself with smiles:
In whose new eyes I know no heaven of tears,
  But still serene desire and between whiles
So great a look that even April's grace
Makes only marvel at her only face.

MAY

This is the laughing-eyed amongst them all:
  My lady's month. A season of young things.
  She rules the light with harmony, and brings
The year's first green upon the beeches tall.
How often, where long creepers wind and fall
  Through the deep woods in noonday wanderings,
  I've heard the month, when she to echo sings,
I've heard the month make merry madrigal.

How often, bosomed in the breathing strong
  Of mosses and young flowerets, have I lain
And watched the clouds, and caught the sheltered song –
  Which it were more than life to hear again –
Of those small birds that pipe it all day long
  Nor far from Marly by the memoried Seine.

JUNE

Rise up and do begin the day's adorning;
The Summer dark is but the dawn of day.
The last of sunset fades into the morning;
The morning calls you from the dark away.
The holy mist, the white mist of morning
Was wreathing upward on my lonely way.
The way was waiting for your own adorning
That should complete the broad adornéd day.

Rise up and do begin the day's adorning;
The little eastern clouds are dapple grey:
There will be wind among the leaves today;
It is the very promise of the morning.
  Lux Tua Vita Mea: your light's my way –
  Then do rise up and make it perfect day.

The Kings come riding back from the Crusade
　　The purple Kings and all their mounted men;
They fill the street with clamorous cavalcade;
　　The Kings have broken down the Saracen.
Singing a great song of the eastern wars,
　　In crimson ships across the sea they came,
With crimson sails and diamonded dark oars,
　　That made the Mediterranean flash with flame.

And reading how, in that far month, the ranks
　　Formed on the edge of the desert, armoured all,
　　　I wish to God that I had been with them
　　When the first Norman leapt upon the wall,
And Godfrey led the foremost of the Franks,
　　And young Lord Raymond stormed Jerusalem.

AUGUST

The soldier month, the bulwark of the year,
　　That never more shall hear such victories told;
He stands apparent with his heaven-high spear,
　　And helmeted of grand Etruscan gold.
Our harvest is the bounty he has won,
　　The loot his fiery temper takes by strength.
Oh! Paladin of the Imperial sun!
　　Oh! crown of all the seasons come at length!

This is sheer manhood; this is Charlemagne,
　　When he with his wide host came conquering home
From vengeance under Roncesvalles ta'en.
　　Or when his bramble beard flaked red with foam
Of bivouac wine-cups on the Lombard plain,
　　What time he swept to grasp the world at Rome.

I, from a window where the Meuse is wide,
   Looked eastward out to the September night;
The men that in the hopeless battle died
   Rose, and reformed, and marshalled for the fight;
A brumal army, vague and ordered large
   For mile on mile by one pale general;
I saw them lean by companies to the charge,
   But no man living heard the bugle-call.

And fading still, and pointing to their scars,
   They rose in lessening cloud, where grey and high
Dawn lay along the heaven in misty bars;
   But watching from that eastern casement, I
   Saw the Republic splendid in the sky,
And round her terrible head the morning stars.

Look, how those steep woods on the mountain's face
   Burn, burn against the sunset; now the cold
   Invades our very noon; the year's grown old,
Mornings are dark, and evenings come apace.
The vines below have lost their purple grace,
   And in Forrèze the white wrack backward rolled
   Hangs to the hills tempestuous, fold on fold,
And moaning gusts make desolate all the place.

Mine host the month, at thy good hostelry,
   Tired limbs I'll stretch and steaming beast I'll tether;
Pile on great logs with Gascon hand and free,
   And pour the Gascon stuff that laughs at weather;
Swell your tough lungs, north wind, no whit care we,
   Singing old songs and drinking wine together.

NOVEMBER

November is that historied Emperor,
   Conquered in age but foot to foot with fate,
Who from his refuge high has heard the roar
   Of squadrons in pursuit, and now, too late,
Stirrups the storm and calls the winds to war,
   And arms the garrison of his last heirloom,
And shakes the sky to its extremest shore
   With battle against irrevocable doom.

Till, driven and hurled from his strong citadels,
   He flies in hurrying cloud and spurs him on,
Empty of lingerings, empty of farewells
   And final benedictions, and is gone.
But in my garden all the trees have shed
Their legacies of the light and all the flowers are dead.

DECEMBER

Hoar Time about the House betakes him slow
Seeking an entry for his weariness.
And in that dreadful company distress
And the sad night with silent footsteps go.
On my poor fire the brands are scarce aglow
And in the woods without what memories press
Where, waning in the trees from less to less,
Mysterious hangs the hornéd moon and low.

For now December, full of agéd care,
Comes in upon the year and weakly grieves;
Mumbling his lost desires and his despair
And with mad trembling hand still interweaves
The dank sear flower-stalks tangled in his hair,
While round about him whirl the rotten leaves.

2

LYRICAL, DIDACTIC AND GROTESQUE

To Dives

Dives, when you and I go down to Hell,
Where scribblers end and millionaires as well,
We shall be carrying on our separate backs
Two very large but very different packs;
And as you stagger under yours, my friend,
Down the dull shore where all our journeys end,
And go before me (as your rank demands)
Towards the infinite flat underlands,
And that dear river of forgetfulness –
Charon, a man of exquisite address
(For, as your wife's progenitors could tell,
They're very strict on etiquette in Hell),
Will, since you are a lord, observe, 'My lord,
We cannot take these weighty things aboard!'
Then down they go, my wretched Dives, down –
The fifteen sorts of boots you kept for town;
The hat to meet the Devil in; the plain
But costly ties; the cases of champagne;
The solid watch, and seal, and chain, and charm;
The working model of a Burning Farm
(To give the little Belials); all the three
Biscuits for Cerberus; the guarantee
From Lambeth that the Rich can never burn,
And even promising a safe return;
The admirable overcoat, designed
To cross Cocytus – very warmly lined:
Sweet Dives, you will leave them all behind
And enter Hell as tattered and as bare
As was your father when he took the air
Behind a barrow-load in Leicester Square.
Then turned to me, and noting one that brings
With careless step a mist of shadowy things:
Laughter and memories, and a few regrets,
Some honour, and a quantity of debts,
A doubt or two of sorts, a trust in God,
And (what will seem to you extremely odd)

His father's granfer's father's father's name,
Unspoilt, untitled, even spelt the same;
Charon, who twenty thousand times before
Has ferried Poets to the ulterior shore,
Will estimate the weight I bear, and cry –
'Comrade!' (He has himself been known to try
His hand at Latin and Italian verse,
Much in the style of Virgil – only worse)
'We let such vain imaginaries pass!'
Then tell me, Dives, which will look the ass –
You, or myself? Or Charon? Who can tell?
They order things so damnably in Hell.

Stanzas written on Battersea Bridge during a South-Westerly Gale

The woods and downs have caught the mid-December,
  The noisy woods and high sea-downs of home;
The wind has found me and I do remember
  The strong scent of the foam.

Woods, darlings of my wandering feet, another
  Possesses you, another treads the Down;
The South-West Wind that was my elder brother
  Has come to me in town.

The wind is shouting from the hills of morning,
  I do remember and I will not stay.
I'll take the Hampton road without a warning
  And get me clean away.

The channel is up, the little seas are leaping,
  The tide is making over Arun Bar;
And there's my boat, where all the rest are sleeping
  And my companions are.

I'll board her, and apparel her, and I'll mount her,
  My boat, that was the strongest friend to me –
That brought my boyhood to its first encounter
  And taught me the wide sea.

Now shall I drive her, roaring hard a' weather,
  Right for the salt and leave them all behind;
We'll quite forget the treacherous streets together
  And find – or shall we find?

There is no Pilotry my soul relies on
  Whereby to catch beneath my bended hand
Faint and beloved along the extreme horizon
  That unforgotten land.

We shall not round the granite piers and paven
  To lie to wharves we know with canvas furled,
My little Boat, we shall not make the haven –
  It is not of the world.

Somewhere of English forelands grandly guarded
  It stands, but not for exiles, marked and clean;
Oh! not for us. A mist has risen and marred it:
  My youth lies in between.

So in this snare that holds me and appals me,
  Where honour hardly lives nor loves remain,
The Sea compels me and my County calls me,
  But stronger things restrain.

          .   .   .   .   .

England, to me that never have malingered,
  Nor spoken falsely, nor your flattery used,
Nor even in my rightful garden lingered:
  What have you not refused?

The South Country

When I am living in the Midlands
    That are sodden and unkind,
I light my lamp in the evening:
    My work is left behind;
And the great hills of the South Country
    Come back into my mind.

The great hills of the South Country
    They stand along the sea;
And it's there walking in the high woods
    That I could wish to be,
And the men that were boys when I was a boy
    Walking along with me.

The men that live in North England
    I saw them for a day:
Their hearts are set upon the waste fells,
    Their skies are fast and grey;
From their castle-walls a man may see
    The mountains far away.

The men that live in West England
    They see the Severn strong,
A-rolling on rough water brown
    Light aspen leaves along.
They have the secret of the Rocks,
    And the oldest kind of song.

But the men that live in the South Country
    Are the kindest and most wise,
They get their laughter from the loud surf,
    And the faith in their happy eyes
Comes surely from our Sister the Spring
    When over the sea she flies;
The violets suddenly bloom at her feet,
    She blesses us with surprise.

I never get between the pines
  But I smell the Sussex air;
Nor I never come on a belt of sand
  But my home is there.
And along the sky the line of the Downs
  So noble and so bare.

A lost thing could I never find,
  Nor a broken thing mend:
And I fear I shall be all alone
  When I get towards the end.
Who will there be to comfort me
  Or who will be my friend?

I will gather and carefully make my friends
  Of the men of the Sussex Weald,
They watch the stars from silent folds,
  They stiffly plough the field.
By them and the God of the South Country
  My poor soul shall be healed.

If I ever become a rich man,
  Or if ever I grow to be old,
I will build a house with deep thatch
  To shelter me from the cold,
And there shall the Sussex songs be sung
  And the story of Sussex told.

I will hold my house in the high wood
  Within a walk of the sea,
And the men that were boys when I was a boy
  Shall sit and drink with me.

The Fanatic

Last night in Compton Street, Soho,
A man whom many of you know
Gave up the ghost at half past nine.
That evening he had been to dine
At Gressington's – an act unwise,
But not the cause of his demise.
The doctors all agree that he
Was touched with cardiac atrophy
Accelerated (more or less)
By lack of proper food, distress,
Uncleanliness, and loss of sleep.
   He was a man that could not keep
His money (when he had the same)
Because of creditors who came
And took it from him; and he gave
So freely that he could not save.
   But all the while a sort of whim
Persistently remained with him,
Half admirable, half absurd:
To keep his word, to keep his word. . . .
By which he did not mean what you
And I would mean (of payments due
Or punctual rental of the Flat –
He was a deal too mad for that)
But – as he put it with a fine
Abandon, foolish or divine –
But 'That great word which every man
Gave God before his life began.'
It was a sacred word, he said,
Which comforted the pathless dead
And made God smile when it was shown
Unforfeited, before the Throne.
And this (he said) he meant to hold
In spite of debt, and hate, and cold;
And this (he said) he meant to show
As passport to the Wards below.

He boasted of it and gave praise
To his own self through all his days.

He wrote a record to preserve
How steadfastly he did not swerve
From keeping it; how stiff he stood
Its guardian, and maintained it good.
He had two witnesses to swear
He kept it once in Berkeley Square.
(Where hardly anything survives)
And, through the loneliest of lives
He kept it clean, he kept it still,
Down to the last extremes of ill.

So when he died, of many friends
Who came in crowds from all the ends
Of London, that it might be known
They knew the man who died alone,
Some, who had thought his mood sublime
And sent him soup from time to time,
Said, 'Well, you cannot make them fit
The world, and there's an end of it!'
But others, wondering at him, said:
'The man that kept his word is dead!'

Then angrily, a certain third
Cried, 'Gentlemen, he kept his word.
And as a man whom beasts surround
Tumultuous, on a little mound
Stands Archer, for one dreadful hour,
Because a Man is born to Power –
And still, to daunt the pack below,
Twangs the clear purpose of his bow,
Till overwhelmed he dares to fall:
So stood this bulwark of us all.
He kept his word as none but he
Could keep it, and as did not we.
And round him as he kept his word
Today's diseased and faithless herd,
A moment loud, a moment strong,
But foul forever, rolled along.'

Courtesy

Of Courtesy, it is much less
Than Courage of Heart or Holiness,
Yet in my Walks it seems to me
That the Grace of God is in Courtesy.

On Monks I did in Storrington fall,
They took me straight into their Hall;
I saw Three Pictures on a wall,
And Courtesy was in them all.

The first the Annunciation;
The second the Visitation;
The third the Consolation,
Of God that was Our Lady's Son.

The first was of Saint Gabriel;
On Wings a-flame from Heaven he fell;
And as he went upon one knee
He shone with Heavenly Courtesy.

Our Lady out of Nazareth rode –
It was Her month of heavy load;
Yet was Her face both great and kind,
For Courtesy was in Her Mind.

The third it was our Little Lord,
Whom all the Kings in arms adored;
He was so small you could not see
His large intent of Courtesy.

Our Lord, that was Our Lady's Son,
Go bless you, People, one by one;
My Rhyme is written, my work is done.

Our Lord and Our Lady

They warned Our Lady for the Child
That was Our blessed Lord,
And She took Him into the desert wild,
   Over the camel's ford.

And a long song She sang to Him
   And a short story told:
And She wrapped Him in a woollen cloak
   To keep Him from the cold.

But when Our Lord was grown a man
   The Rich they dragged Him down,
And they crucified Him in Golgotha,
   Out and beyond the Town.

They crucified Him on Calvary,
   Upon an April day;
And because He had been her little Son
   She followed Him all the way.

Our Lady stood beside the Cross,
   A little space apart,
And when She heard Our Lord cry out
   A sword went through Her Heart.

They laid Our Lord in a marble tomb,
   Dead, in a winding sheet.
But Our Lady stands above the world
   With the white Moon at Her feet.

The Night

Most holy Night, that still dost keep
The keys of all the doors of sleep,
To me when my tired eyelids close
    Give thou repose.

And let the far lament of them
That chaunt the dead day's requiem
Make in my ears, who wakeful lie,
    Soft lullaby.

Let them that guard the hornéd moon
By my bedside their memories croon.
So shall I have new dreams and blest
    In my brief rest.

Fold your great wings about my face,
Hide dawning from my resting-place,
And cheat me with your false delight,
    Most Holy Night.

The Early Morning

The moon on the one hand, the dawn on the other:
The moon is my sister, the dawn is my brother.
The moon on my left and the dawn on my right.
My brother, good morning: my sister, good night.

The Leader

The sword fell down: I heard a knell;
  I thought that ease was best,
And sullen men that buy and sell
  Were host: and I was guest.
All unashamed I sat with swine,
  We shook the dice for war,
The night was drunk with an evil wine –
  But she went on before.

    She rode a steed of the sea-foam breed,
      All faery was her blade,
    And the armour on her tender limbs
      Was of the moonshine made.

By God that sends the master-maids,
  I know not whence she came,
But the sword she bore to save the soul
  Went up like an altar flame
Where a broken race in a desert place
  Call on the Holy Name.

    We strained our eyes in the dim day-rise,
      We could not see them plain;
    But two dead men from Valmy fen
      Rode at her bridle-rein.

I hear them all, my fathers call,
  I see them how they ride,
And where had been that rout obscene
  Was an army straight with pride.
A hundred thousand marching men,
  Of squadrons twenty score,
And after them all the guns, the guns,
  But she went on before.

Her face was like a king's command
When all the swords are drawn.
She stretched her arms and smiled at us,
Her head was higher than the hills.
She led us to the endless plains.
We lost her in the dawn.

A Bivouac

I

You came without a human sound,
   You came and brought my soul to me;
I only woke, and all around
They slumbered on the firelit ground,
   Beside the guns in Burgundy.

II

I felt the gesture of your hands,
   You signed my forehead with the Cross;
The gesture of your holy hands
Was bounteous – like the misty lands
   Along the Hills in Calvados.

III

But when I slept I saw your eyes,
   Hungry as death, and very far.
I saw demand in your dim eyes
Mysterious as the moons that rise
   At midnight, in the Pines of Var.

To the Balliol Men still in Africa

Years ago when I was at Balliol,
   Balliol men – and I was one –
Swam together in winter rivers,
   Wrestled together under the sun.
And still in the heart of us, Balliol, Balliol,
   Loved already, but hardly known,
Welded us each of us into the others:
   Called a levy and chose her own.

Here is a House that armours a man
   With the eyes of a boy and the heart of a ranger
And a laughing way in the teeth of the world
   And a holy hunger and thirst for danger:
Balliol made me, Balliol fed me,
   Whatever I had she gave me again:
And the best of Balliol loved and led me.
   God be with you, Balliol men.

I have said it before, and I say it again,
   There was treason done, and a false word spoken,
And England under the dregs of men,
   And bribes about, and a treaty broken;
But angry, lonely, hating it still,
   I wished to be there in spite of the wrong.
My heart was heavy for Cumnor Hill
   And the hammer of galloping all day long.

Galloping outward into the weather,
   Hands a-ready and battle in all:
Words together and wine together
   And song together in Balliol Hall.
Rare and single! Noble and few! . . .
   Oh! they have wasted you over the sea!
The only brothers ever I knew,
   The men that laughed and quarrelled with me.

     .   .   .   .   .   .

Balliol made me, Balliol fed me,
  Whatever I had she gave me again;
And the best of Balliol loved and led me.
  God be with you, Balliol men.

An Oracle

Matutinus adest ubi Vesper, et accipiens te
Saepe recusatum voces intelligit hospes
Rusticus ignotas notas, ac flumina tellus
Occupat – In sancto tum, tum, stans Aede caveto
Tonsuram Hirsuti Capitis, via namque pedestrem
Ferrea praeveniens cursum, peregrine, laborem
Pro pietate tua inceptum frustratur, amore
Antiqui Ritus alto sub Numine Romae.

Translation of the above:

When early morning seems but eve
And they that still refuse receive:
When speech unknown men understand;
And floods are crossed upon dry land.
Within the Sacred Walls beware
The Shaven Head that boasts of Hair,
For when the road attains the rail
The Pilgrim's great attempt shall fail.

Verses to a Lord who, in the House of Lords,
said that those who opposed the
South African Adventure confused Soldiers
with Money-Grubbers

You thought because we held, my lord,
  An ancient cause and strong,
That therefore we maligned the sword:
  My lord, you did us wrong.

We also know the sacred height
  Up on Tugela side,
Where those three hundred fought with Beit
  And fair young Wernher died.

The daybreak on the failing force,
  The final sabres drawn:
Tall Goltman, silent on his horse,
  Superb against the dawn.

The little mound where Eckstein stood
  And gallant Albu fell,
And Oppenheim, half blind with blood
Went fording through the rising flood –
  My Lord, we know them well.

The little empty homes forlorn,
The ruined synagogues that mourn,
  In Frankfort and Berlin;
We knew them when the peace was torn –
We of a nobler lineage born –
And now by all the gods of scorn
  We mean to rub them in.

The Rebel

There is a wall of which the stones
Are lies and bribes and dead men's bones.
And wrongfully this evil wall
Denies what all men made for all,
And shamelessly this wall surrounds
Our homesteads and our native grounds.

But I will gather and I will ride,
And I will summon a countryside,
And many a man shall hear my halloa
Who never had thought the horn to follow:
And many a man shall ride with me
Who never had thought on earth to see
High Justice in her armoury.

When we find them where they stand,
A mile of men on either hand,
I mean to charge from right away
And force the flanks of their array,
And press them inward from the plains,
And drive them clamouring down the lanes,
And gallop and harry and have them down,
And carry the gates and hold the town.
Then shall I rest me from my ride
With my great anger satisfied.

Only, before I eat and drink,
When I have killed them all, I think
That I will batter their carven names,
And slit the pictures in their frames,
And burn for scent their cedar door,
And melt the gold their women wore,
And hack their horses at the knees,
And hew to death their timber trees,
And plough their gardens deep and through –
And all these things I mean to do
For fear perhaps my little son
Should break his hands, as I have done.

Homage

There is a light around your head
Which only Saints of God may wear,
And all the flowers on which you tread
In pleasaunce more than ours have fed,
And supped the essential air
Whose summer is a-pulse with music everywhere.

For you are younger than the mornings are
That in the mountains break;
When upland shepherds see their only star
Pale on the dawn, and make
In his surcease the hours,
The early hours of all their happy circuit take.

The Prophet Lost in the Hills at Evening

Strong God which made the topmost stars
    To circulate and keep their course,
Remember me; whom all the bars
    Of sense and dreadful fate enforce.

Above me in your heights and tall,
    Impassable the summits freeze,
Below the haunted waters call
    Impassable beyond the trees.

I hunger and I have no bread.
    My gourd is empty of the wine.
Surely the footsteps of the dead
    Are shuffling softly close to mine!

It darkens. I have lost the ford.
    There is a change on all things made.
The rocks have evil faces, Lord,
    And I am awfully afraid.

Remember me: The Voids of Hell
    Expand enormous all around.
Strong friend of souls, Emmanuel,
    Redeem me from accurséd ground.

The long descent of wasted days,
    To these at last have led me down;
Remember that I filled with praise
The meaningless and doubtful ways
    That lead to an eternal town.

I challenged and I kept the Faith,
    The bleeding path alone I trod;
It darkens. Stand about my wraith,
    And harbour me – almighty God.

The End of the Road

In these boots and with this staff
Two hundred leaguers and a half
Walked I, went I, paced I, tripped I,
Marched I, held I, skelped I, slipped I,
Pushed I, panted, swung and dashed I;
Picked I, forded, swam and splashed I,
Strolled I, climbed I, crawled and scrambled,
Dropped and dipped I, ranged and rambled;
Plodded I, hobbled I, trudged and tramped I,
And in lonely spinnies camped I,
And in haunted pinewoods slept I,
Lingered, loitered, limped and crept I,
Clambered, halted, stepped and leapt I;
Slowly sauntered, roundly strode I,
And . . .   (Oh! Patron saints and Angels
            That protect the four Evangels!
            And you Prophets vel majores
            Vel incerti, vel minores,
            Virgines ac confessores
            Chief of whose peculiar glories
            Est in Aula Regis stare
            Atque orare et exorare
            Et clamare et conclamare
            Clamantes cum clamoribus
            Pro Nobis Peccatoribus.)
Let me not conceal it. . . . *Rode I.*
(For who but critics could complain
Of 'riding' in a railway train?)
Across the valleys and the high-land,
With all the world on either hand
Drinking when I had a mind to,
Singing when I felt inclined to;
Nor ever turned my face to home
  Till I had slaked my heart at Rome.

The Moon's Funeral

I

The Moon is dead. I saw her die.
She in a drifting cloud was drest,
She lay along the uncertain west,
A dream to see.
And very low she spake to me:
'I go where none may understand,
I fade into the nameless land,
And there must lie perpetually.'
And therefore I,
And therefore loudly, loudly I
And high
And very piteously make cry:
'The Moon is dead. I saw her die.'

II

And will she never rise again?
The Holy Moon? Oh, never more!
Perhaps along the inhuman shore
Where pale ghosts are
Beyond the low Lethean fen
She and some wide infernal star . . .
To us who loved her never more,
The Moon will never rise again.
Oh! never more in nightly sky
Her eye so high shall peep and pry
To see the great world rolling by.
For why?
The Moon is dead. I saw her die.

The Death and Last Confession of
Wandering Peter

When Peter Wanderwide was young
   He wandered everywhere he would:
And all that he approved was sung,
   And most of what he saw was good.

When Peter Wanderwide was thrown
   By Death himself beyond Auxerre,
He chanted in heroic tone
   To priests and people gathered there:

'If all that I have loved and seen
   Be with me on the Judgement Day,
I shall be saved the crowd between
   From Satan and his foul array.

'Almighty God will surely cry,
   "St Michael! Who is this that stands
With Ireland in his dubious eye,
   And Perigord between his hands,

' "And on his arm the stirrup-thongs,
   And in his gait the narrow seas,
And in his mouth Burgundian songs,
   But in his heart the Pyrenees?"

'St Michael then will answer right
   (And not without angelic shame),
"I seem to know his face by sight:
   I cannot recollect his name . . .?"

'St Peter will befriend me then,
   Because my name is Peter too:
"I know him for the best of men
   That ever walloped barley brew.

' "And though I did not know him well
   And though his soul were clogged with sin,
I hold the keys of Heaven and Hell.
   Be welcome, noble Peterkin."

' Then shall I spread my native wings
    And tread secure the heavenly floor,
And tell the Blessed doubtful things
    Of Val d'Aran and Perigord.'

This was the last and solemn jest
    Of weary Peter Wanderwide.
He spoke it with a failing zest,
    And having spoken it, he died.

The North Sea

The moving mind that God gave me
Is manifold as the wide North Sea,
And as the sea is full of things,
The great fish in their wanderings
And the spread galleys of the old kings
And darkness eddying round in rings,
So, packed with all that I have done
And felt and known and lost and won,
By the tide drifted and the wind inclined
Moves my not measurable mind.

I mean to write with all my strength
   (It lately has been sadly waning),
A ballad of enormous length –
   Some parts of which will need explaining.[1]

Because (unlike the bulk of men
   Who write for fame or public ends),
I turn a lax and fluent pen
   To talking of my private friends.[2]

For no one, in our long decline,
   So dusty, spiteful and divided,
Had quite such pleasant friends as mine,
   Or loved them half as much as I did.

     ·   ·   ·   ·   ·

The Freshman ambles down the High,
   In love with everything he sees,
He notes the racing autumn sky,
   He sniffs a lively autumn breeze.

'Can this be Oxford? This the place?'
   (He cries) 'of which my father said
The tutoring was a damned disgrace,
   The creed a mummery, stuffed and dead?

'Can it be here that Uncle Paul
   Was driven by excessive gloom
To drink and debt, and, last of all,
   To smoking opium in his room?

> 1. But do not think I shall explain
>   To any great extent. Believe me,
> I partly write to give you pain,
>   And if you do not like me, leave me.
>
> 2. And least of all can you complain,
>   Reviewers, whose unholy trade is,
> To puff with all your might and main
>   Biographies of single ladies.

'Is it from here the people come,
    Who talk so loud, and roll their eyes,
And stammer? How extremely rum!
    How curious! What a great surprise!

'Some influence of a nobler day
    Than theirs (I mean than Uncle Paul's),
Has roused the sleep of their decay,
    And flecked with light their crumbling walls.

'O! dear undaunted boys of old,
    Would that your names were carven here,
For all the world in stamps of gold,
    That I might read them and revere.

'Who brought and handed down for me
    This Oxford of the larger air,
Laughing, and full of faith, and free,
    With youth resplendent everywhere?'

Then learn: thou ill-instructed, blind,
    Young, callow, and untutored man,
Their private names were . . . [1]
    Their club was called REPUBLICAN.

. . . . .

Where on their banks of light they lie,
    The happy hills of Heaven between,
The Gods that rule the morning sky
    Are not more young, nor more serene

Than were the intrepid Four that stand,
    The first who dared to live their dream.
And on this uncongenial land
    To found the Abbey of Theleme.

1. Never mind.

We kept the Rabelaisian plan:[1]
   We dignified the dainty cloisters
With Natural Law, the Rights of Man,
   Song, Stoicism, Wine and Oysters.

The library was most inviting:
   The books upon the crowded shelves
Were mainly of our private writing:
   We kept a school and taught ourselves.

We taught the art of writing things
   On men we still should like to throttle:
And where to get the Blood of Kings
   At only half a crown a bottle.

     •   •   •   •

Eheu Fugaces! Postume!
   (An old quotation out of mode);
My coat of dreams is stolen away
   My youth is passing down the road.

     •   •   •   •

The wealth of youth, we spent it well
   And decently, as very few can.
And is it lost? I cannot tell:
   And what is more, I doubt if you can.

The question's very much too wide,
   And much too deep, and much too hollow,
And learned men on either side
   Use arguments I cannot follow.

They say that in the unchanging place,
   Where all we loved is always dear,
We meet our morning face to face
   And find at last our twentieth year. . . .

1. The plan forgot (I know not how,
    Perhaps the Refectory filled it),
To put a chapel in; and now
    We're mortgaging the rest to build it.

They say (and I am glad they say)
   It is so; and it may be so:
It may be just the other way,
   I cannot tell. But this I know:

From quiet homes and first beginning,
   Out to the undiscovered ends,
There's nothing worth the wear of winning,
   But laughter and the love of friends.

    .   .   .   .   .

But something dwindles, oh! my peers,
   And something cheats the heart and passes,
And Tom that meant to shake the years
   Has come to merely rattling glasses.

And He, the Father of the Flock,
   Is keeping Burmesans in order,
An exile on a lonely rock
   That overlooks the Chinese border.

And One (Myself I mean – no less),
   Ah! – will Posterity believe it –
Not only don't deserve success,
   But hasn't managed to achieve it.

Not even this peculiar town
   Has ever fixed a friendship firmer,
But – one is married, one's gone down,
   And one's a Don, and one's in Burmah.

    .   .   .   .   .

And oh! the days, the days, the days,
   When all the four were off together:
The infinite deep of summer haze,
   The roaring boast of autumn weather!

    .   .   .   .   .

I will not try the reach again,
   I will not set my sail alone,
To moor a boat bereft of men
   At Yarnton's tiny docks of stone.

But I will sit beside the fire,
　And put my hand before my eyes,
And trace, to fill my heart's desire,
　The last of all our Odysseys.

The quiet evening kept her tryst:
　Beneath an open sky we rode,
And passed into a wandering mist
　Along the perfect Evenlode.

The tender Evenlode that makes
　Her meadows hush to hear the sound
Of waters mingling in the brakes,
　And binds my heart to English ground.

A lovely river, all alone,
　She lingers in the hills and holds
A hundred little towns of stone,
　Forgotten in the western wolds.

　　．　　．　　．　　．　　．

I dare to think (though meaner powers
　Possess our thrones, and lesser wits
Are drinking worser wine than ours,
　In what's no longer Austerlitz).

That surely a tremendous ghost,
　The brazen-lunged, the bumper-filler,
Still sings to an immortal toast,
　The Misadventures of the Miller.

The unending seas are hardly bar
　To men with such a prepossession:
We were? Why then, by God, we *are* –
　Order! I call the Club to session!

You do retain the song we set,
　And how it rises, trips and scans?
You keep the sacred memory yet,
　Republicans? Republicans?

You know the way the words were hurled,
    To break the worst of fortune's rub?
I give the toast across the world,
    And drink it, 'Gentlemen: the Club.'

Dedication on the Gift of a Book to a Child

Child! do not throw this book about!
    Refrain from the unholy pleasure
Of cutting all the pictures out!
    Preserve it as your chiefest treasure.

Child, have you never heard it said
    That you are heir to all the ages?
Why, then, your hands were never made
    To tear these beautiful thick pages!

Your little hands were made to take
    The better things and leave the worse ones:
They also may be used to shake
    The Massive Paws of Elder Persons.

And when your prayers complete the day,
    Darling, your little tiny hands
Were also made, I think, to pray
    For men that lose their fairylands.

Dedication of a Child's Book of Imaginary Tales

And is it true? It is not true!
And if it was it wouldn't do
For people such as me and you,
Who very nearly all day long
Are doing something rather wrong.

The Happy Journalist

I love to walk about at night
    By nasty lanes and corners foul,
All shielded from the unfriendly light
    And independent as the owl.

By dirty grates I love to lurk;
    I often stoop to take a squint
At printers working at their work.
    I muse upon the rot they print.

The beggars please me, and the mud:
    The editors beneath their lamps
As – Mr Howl demanding blood,
    And Lord Retender stealing stamps,

And Mr Bing instructing liars,
    His elder son composing trash;
Beaufort (whose real name is Meyers)
    Refusing anything but cash.

I like to think of Mr Meyers,
    I like to think of Mr Bing.
I like to think about the liars:
    It pleases me, that sort of thing.

Policemen speak to me, but I,
    Remembering my civic rights,
Neglect them and do not reply.
    I love to walk about at nights!

At twenty-five to four I bunch
    Across a cab I can't afford.
I ring for breakfast after lunch.
    I am as happy as a lord!

Lines to a Don

Remote and ineffectual Don
That dared attack my Chesterton,
With that poor weapon, half-impelled,
Unlearnt, unsteady, hardly held,
Unworthy for a tilt with men –
Your quavering and corroded pen;
Don poor at Bed and worse at Table,
Don pinched, Don starved, Don miserable;
Don stuttering, Don with roving eyes,
Don nervous, Don of crudities;
Don clerical, Don ordinary,
Don self-absorbed and solitary;
Don here-and-there, Don epileptic;
Don puffed and empty, Don dyspeptic;
Don middle-class, Don sycophantic,
Don dull, Don brutish, Don pedantic;
Don hypocritical, Don bad,
Don furtive, Don three-quarters mad;
Don (since a man must make an end),
Don that shall never be my friend.

  . . . . .

Don different from those regal Dons!
With hearts of gold and lungs of bronze,
Who shout and bang and roar and bawl
The Absolute across the hall,
Or sail in amply bellying gown
Enormous through the Sacred Town,
Bearing from College to their homes
Deep cargoes of gigantic tomes;
Dons admirable! Dons of Might!
Uprising on my inward sight
Compact of ancient tales, and port
And sleep – and learning of a sort.
Dons English, worthy of the land;
Dons rooted; Dons that understand.

Good Dons perpetual that remain
A landmark, walling in the plain –
The horizon of my memories –
Like large and comfortable trees.

· · · · ·

Don very much apart from these,
Thou scapegoat Don, thou Don devoted,
Don to thine own damnation quoted,
Perplexed to find thy trivial name
Reared in my verse to lasting shame.
Don dreadful, rasping Don and wearing,
Repulsive Don – Don past all bearing.
Don of the cold and doubtful breath,
Don despicable, Don of death;
Don nasty, skimpy, silent, level;
Don evil; Don that serves the devil,
Don ugly – that makes fifty lines.
There is a Canon which confines
A Rhymed Octosyllabic Curse
If written in Iambic Verse
To fifty lines. I never cut;
I far prefer to end it – but
Believe me I shall soon return.
My fires are banked, but still they burn
To write some more about the Don
That dared attack my Chesterton.

Newdigate Poem

A PRIZE POEM SUBMITTED BY MR LAMBKIN,
THEN SCHOLAR AND LATER FELLOW OF
BURFORD COLLEGE,
TO THE EXAMINERS OF THE UNIVERSITY OF OXFORD
ON THE PRESCRIBED POETIC THEME
SET BY THEM IN 1893,
'THE BENEFITS OF THE ELECTRIC LIGHT'

Hail, Happy Muse, and touch the tuneful string!
The benefits conferred by Science[1] I sing.
Under the kind Examiners' direction[2]
I only write about them in connection
With benefits which the Electric Light
  Confers on us; especially at night.
These are my theme, of these my song shall rise.
My lofty head shall swell to strike the skies.[3]
And tears of hopeless love bedew the maiden's eyes.
    Descend, O Muse, from thy divine abode,
    To Osney, on the Seven Bridges Road;
For under Osney's solitary shade
The bulk of the Electric Light is made.
Here are the works; – from hence the current flows
Which (so the Company's prospectus goes)
    Can furnish to Subscribers hour by hour
No less than sixteen thousand candle power,[4]
All at a thousand volts. (It is essential
To keep the current at this high potential
In spite of the considerable expense.)
    The Energy developed represents,
Expressed in foot-tons, the united forces
Of fifteen elephants and forty horses.

1. To be pronounced as a monosyllable in the Imperial fashion.
2. Mr Punt, Mr Howl, and Mr Grewcock (now, alas, deceased).
3. A neat rendering of 'Sublimi feriam sidera vertice'.
4. To the Examiners: These facts (of which I guarantee the accuracy) were given me by a Director.

But shall my scientific detail thus
Clip the dear wings of Buoyant Pegasus?
    Shall pure statistics jar upon the ear
That pants for Lyric accents loud and clear?
Shall I describe the complex Dynamo
Or write about its Commutator? No!
    To happier fields I lead my wanton pen,
The proper study of mankind is men.
    Awake, my Muse! Portray the pleasing sight
That meets us where they make Electric Light.
    Behold the Electrician where he stands:
Soot, oil, and verdigris are on his hands;
Large spots of grease defile his dirty clothes,
The while his conversation drips with oaths.
Shall such a being perish in its youth?
Alas! it is indeed the fatal truth.
In that dull brain, beneath that hair unkempt,
Familiarity has bred contempt.
We warn him of the gesture all too late:
Oh, Heartless Jove! Oh, Adamantine Fate!
    A random touch – a hand's imprudent slip –
The Terminals – a flash – a sound like 'Zip!' –
A smell of burning fills the startled Air –
The Electrician is no longer there!
    But let us turn with true Artistic scorn
From facts funereal and from views forlorn
Of Erebus and Blackest midnight born.[1]
    Arouse thee, Muse! and chaunt in accents rich
The interesting processes by which
The Electricity is passed along;
These are my theme: to these I bend my song.
    It runs encased in wood or porous brick
Through copper wires two millimetres thick,
And insulated on their dangerous mission
By indiarubber, silk, or composition.
Here you may put with critical felicity
The following question: 'What is Electricity?'

1. A reminiscence of Milton: 'fas est et ab hoste doceri'.

'Molecular Activity,' say some,
Others when asked say nothing, and are dumb.
Whatever be its nature, this is clear:
The rapid current checked in its career,
Baulked in its race and halted in its course[1]
Transforms to heat and light its latent force:

It needs no pedant in the lecturer's chair
To prove that light and heat are present there.
The pear-shaped vacuum globe, I understand,
Is far too hot to fondle with the hand.
While, as is patent to the meanest sight,
The carbon filament is very bright.

As for the lights they hang about the town,
Some praise them highly, others run them down.
This system (technically called the Arc),
Makes some passages too light, others too dark.

But in the house the soft and constant rays
Have always met with universal praise.

For instance: if you want to read in bed
No candle burns beside your curtain's head,
For from some distant corner of the room
The incandescent lamp dispels the gloom,
And with the largest print need hardly try
The powers of any young and vigorous eye.

Aroint thee, Muse! Inspired the poet sings!
I cannot help observing future things!
Life is a vale, its paths are dark and rough
Only because we do not know enough:
When Science has discovered something more
We shall be happier than we were before.

Hail, Britain, Mistress of the Azure Main,
Ten thousand Fleets swoop over thee in vain!
Hail, Mighty Mother of the Brave and Free,
That beat Napoleon, and gave birth to me!

---

1. Lambkin told me he regretted this line, which was for the sake of Rhyme. He would willingly have replaced it, but to his last day could construct no substitute.

Thou that canst wrap in thine emblazoned robe
One quarter of the habitable globe.
Thy mountains, wafted by a favouring breeze,
Like mighty rocks withstand the stormy seas.

    Thou art a Christian Commonwealth, and yet
Be thou not all unthankful – nor forget
As thou exultest in Imperial Might
The Benefits of the Electric Light.

The Yellow Mustard

Oh! ye that prink it to and fro,
In pointed flounce and furbelow,
What have ye known, what can ye know
That have not seen the mustard grow?

The yellow mustard is no less
Than God's good gift to loneliness;
And he was sent in gorgeous press
To jangle keys at my distress.

I heard the throstle call again,
Come hither, Pain! come hither, Pain!
Till all my shameless feet were fain
To wander through the summer rain.

And far apart from human place,
And flaming like a vast disgrace,
There struck me blinding in the face
The livery of the mustard race.

.   .   .   .   .

To see the yellow mustard grow
Beyond the town, above, below;
Beyond the purple houses, oh!
To see the yellow mustard grow!

The Politician or the Irish Earldom

A strong and striking Personality,
　　Worth several hundred thousand pounds –
Of strict political Morality –
　　Was walking in his park-like Grounds;
When, just as these began to pall on him
　　(I mean the Trees, and Things like that),
A Person who had come to call on him
　　Approached him, taking off his Hat.

He said, with singular veracity:
　　'I serve our Sea-girt Mother-Land
In no conspicuous capacity.
　　I am but an Attorney; and
I do a little elementary
　　Negotiation, now and then,
As Agent for a Parliamentary
　　Division of the Town of N. . . .

'Merely as one of the Electorate –
　　A member of the Commonweal –
Before completing my Directorate,
　　I want to know the way you feel,
On matters more or less debatable;
　　As – whether our Imperial Pride
Can treat as taxable or rateable
　　The Gardens of . . . ' His host replied:

'The Ravages of Inebriety
　　(Alas! increasing day by day!)
Are undermining all Society.
　　I do not hesitate to say
My country squanders her abilities;
　　Observe how Montenegro treats
Her Educational Facilities. . . .
　　. . . As to the African defeats,

92

'I bitterly deplored their frequency;
   On Canada we are agreed,
The Laws protecting Public Decency
   Are very, very lax indeed!
The Views of most of the Nobility
   Are very much the same as mine,
On Thingumbob's eligibility . . .
   I trust that you remain to dine?'

His Lordship pressed with importunity,
   As rarely he had pressed before.
         .   .   .   .   .

It gave them both an opportunity
   To know each other's value more.

Eheu! Fugaces

Two years ago, or it may be three,
Lord! how time passes,
Especially with me!
Eheu fugaces!
May we not play in the woods again,
Lads to the lasses!
Must we be men?
Eheu fugaces!
Still blows the wind and the rain comes down
All the window glasses
Of this dirty town.
Eheu fugaces!

The Loser

He lost his money first of all
   – And losing that is half the story –
And later on he tried a fall
   With Fate, in things less transitory.

He lost his heart – and found it dead –
   (His one and only true discovery),
And after that he lost his head,
   And lost his chances of recovery.

He lost his honour bit by bit
   Until the thing was out of question.
He worried so at losing it,
   He lost his sleep and his digestion.

He lost his temper – and for good –
   The remnants of his reputation,
His taste in wine, his choice of food,
   And then, in rapid culmination,

His certitudes, his sense of truth,
   His memory, his self-control,
The love that graced his early youth,
   And lastly his immortal soul.

Twelfth Night

As I was lifting over Down
A winter's night to Petworth Town,
I came upon a company
Of Travellers who would talk with me.

The riding moon was small and bright,
They cast no shadows in her light:
There was no man for miles a-near.
I would not walk with them for fear.

A star in heaven by Gumber glowed,
An ox across the darkness lowed,
Whereat a burning light there stood
Right in the heart of Gumber Wood.

Across the rime their marching rang,
And in a little while they sang;
They sang a song I used to know,
Gloria In Excelsis Domino.

The frozen way those people trod
It led towards the Mother of God;
Perhaps if I had travelled with them
I might have come to Bethlehem.

The Seasons

They whom their mothers bare through Summer heat,
Are boys of Autumn, and a fruit complete.

They whom their mothers bare through April rain,
Are new as April, and as April vain.

They whom their mothers in dark Winters bare,
Wake to a barren world, and straight despair.

But they that held through Winter to the Spring
Despair as I do, and, as I do, sing.

Down Channel

The Channel pours out on the Ebb in a river gigantic.
  There is no Moon.
The Dark is low in a cloud on the huge Atlantic.
  We'll be raising the Lizard soon.

There will be no meeting of eyes, nor any blessing,
  After the run.
The lips are still and the hand has ceased from caressing.
  There is nothing more to be done.

To the Eighth Regiment of Artillery in the French Service now in Garrison at Nancy

Freedom is up for sale and all assess her;
The Tyrants have put in their ancient pleas;
The Usurers are the heirs of the Oppressor;
The insolent boast of Hell is on the High Seas.

The Sword that was the strength of the poor is broken;
The wrath that was the wealth of the poor is spent;
Witless are all the great words we have spoken –
But you, my regiment?

You that put down the mighty from their seat,
And fought to fill the hungry with good things,
And turned the rich men empty to the street,
And trailed your scabbards in the halls of Kings.

Do you remember how you cleared the timber
At Leipzig, holding an unequal fight,
Or heard Ney shouting for the guns to unlimber,
And hold the Beresina Bridge at night?

Do you remember the immortal chorus,
In Valmy fog, and where our Captains stood
Till the cannonade had opened the world before us
To the broad daylight and the pride of the Latin blood?

The Sword that was the strength of the poor is broken;
The wrath that was the wealth of the poor is spent;
Witless are all the great words we have spoken –
But you, my regiment?

He does not die that can bequeath
Some influence to the land he knows,
Or dares, persistent, interwreath
Love permanent with the wild hedgerows;
     He does not die, but still remains
     Substantiate with his darling plains.

The spring's superb adventure calls
His dust athwart the woods to flame;
His boundary river's secret falls
Perpetuate and repeat his name.
     He rides his loud October sky:
     He does not die. He does not die.

The beeches know the accustomed head
Which loved them, and a peopled air
Beneath their benediction spread
Comforts the silence everywhere;
     For native ghosts return and these
     Perfect the mystery in the trees.

So, therefore, though myself be crosst
The shuddering of that dreadful day
When friend and fire and home are lost
And even children drawn away –
     The passer-by shall hear me still,
     A boy that sings on Duncton Hill.

My Own Country

I shall go without companions,
  And with nothing in my hand;
I shall pass through many places
  That I cannot understand –
Until I come to my own country,
  Which is a pleasant land!

The trees that grow in my own country
  Are the beech tree and the yew;
Many stand together,
  And some stand few.
In the month of May in my own country
  All the woods are new.

When I get to my own country
  I shall lie down and sleep;
I shall watch in the valleys
  The long flocks of sheep.
And then I shall dream, for ever and all,
  A good dream and deep.

The Desert

I stood in the desert, and I watched the snows
On Aures, in their splendour from the west.
Sahara darkened: and I thought of those
That hold in isolation and are blest.

They that in dereliction grow perfected:
They that are silent: they that stand apart:
They that shall judge the world as God's elected:
They that have had the sword athwart the heart.

Farewell to Juliet

How shall I round the ending of a Story,
    Now the wind's falling and the Harbour nears?
How shall I sign your tiny Book of Glory?
    Juliet, my Juliet, after many years.

I'll sign it, One that halted at a Vision:
    One whom the shaft of Beauty struck to Flame:
One that so wavered in a strong Decision:
    One that was born perhaps to fix your name.

One that was pledged, and goes to his Replevining;
    One that now leaves you with averted Face.
A Shadow passing through the Doors at Evening
    To his Companion and his Resting Place.

3
SONGS

Noël

I

On a winter's night long time ago
    (*The bells ring loud and the bells ring low*),
When high howled wind, and down fell snow
    (Carillon, Carilla).
Saint Joseph he and Nostre Dame,
Riding on an ass, full weary came
From Nazareth into Bethlehem.
      And the small child Jesus smile on you.

II

And Bethlehem inn they stood before
    (*The bells ring less and the bells ring more*),
The landlord bade them begone from his door
    (Carillon, Carilla).
'Poor folk' (says he), 'must lie where they may,
For the Duke of Jewry comes this way,
With all his train on a Christmas Day.'
      And the small child Jesus smile on you.

III

Poor folk that may my carol hear
    (*The bells ring single and the bells ring clear*),
See! God's one child had hardest cheer!
    (Carillon, Carilla).
Men grown hard on a Christmas morn;
The dumb beast by and a babe forlorn.
It was very, very cold when our Lord was born.
      And the small child Jesus smile on you.

IV

Now these were Jews as Jews must be
    (*The bells ring merry and the bells ring free*).
But Christian men in a band are we
    (Carillon, Carilla).

Empty we go, and ill be-dight,
Singing Noël on a Winter's night.
Give us to sup by the warm firelight,
    And the small child Jesus smile on you.

The Birds

When Jesus Christ was four years old,
The angels brought Him toys of gold,
Which no man ever had bought or sold.

And yet with these He would not play.
He made Him small fowl out of clay,
And blessed them till they flew away:
      Tu creasti Domine.

Jesus Christ, Thou child so wise,
Bless mine hands and fill mine eyes,
And bring my soul to Paradise.

In a Boat

Lady! Lady!
Upon Heaven-height,
Above the harsh morning
In the mere light.

Above the spindrift
And above the snow,
Where no seas tumble,
And no winds blow.

The twisting tides,
And the perilous sands
Upon all sides
Are in your holy hands.

The wind harries
And the cold kills;
But I see your chapel
Over far hills.

My body is frozen,
My soul is afraid:
Stretch out your hands to me,
Mother and maid.

Mother of Christ,
And Mother of me,
Save me alive
From the howl of the sea.

If you will Mother me
Till I grow old,
I will hang in your chapel
A ship of pure gold.

Song

I

You wear the morning like your dress
And are with mastery crowned;
Whenas you walk your loveliness
Goes shining all around.
Upon your secret, smiling way
Such new contents were found,
The Dancing Loves made holiday
On that delighted ground.

II

Then summon April forth, and send
Commandment through the flowers;
About our woods your grace extend
A queen of careless hours.
For oh, not Vera veiled in rain,
Nor Dian's sacred Ring,
With all her royal nymphs in train
Could so lead on the Spring.

The Ring

When I was flying before the King
In the wood of Valognes in my hiding,
Although I had not anything
I sent a woman a golden ring.

A Ring of the Moors beyond Leon
With emerald and with diamond stone,
And a writing no man ever had known,
And an opal standing all alone.

The shape of the ring the heart to bind:
The emerald turns from cold to kind:
The writing makes her sure to find: —
But the evil opal changed her mind.

Now when the King was dead, was he,
I came back hurriedly over the sea
From the long rocks in Normandy
To Bosham that is by Selsey.
And we clipt each other knee to knee.
But what I had was lost to me.

Cuckoo!

In woods so long time bare
    Cuckoo!
Up and in the wood, I know not where
Two notes fall.
Yet I do not envy him at all
His phantasy.
Cuckoo!
I too,
Somewhere,
I have sung as merrily as he
Who can dare,
Small and careless lover, so to laugh at care,
And who
Can call
Cuckoo!
In woods of winter weary,
In scented woods, of winter weary, call
Cuckoo!
In woods so long time bare.

The Little Serving Maid

I

There was a Queen of England,
  And a good Queen too.
She had a house in Powis Land
  With the Severn running through;
And Men-folk and Women-folk
  Apprenticed to a trade;
But the prettiest of all
  Was a Little Serving Maid.

II

'Oh Madam, Queen of England!
  Oh will you let me go!
For there's a Lad in London
  And he would have it so.
And I would have it too, Madam,
  And with him would I bide;
And he will be the Groom, Madam,
  And I shall be the Bride!'

III

'Oh fie to you and shame to you,
  You Little Serving Maid!
And are you not astonied?
  And are you not afraid?
For never was it known
  Since Yngelonde began
That a Little Serving Maid
  Should go a-meeting of a man!'

IV

Then the Little Serving Maid
  She went and laid her down,
With her cross and her beads,
  In her new courting gown.

And she called in Mother Mary's name
  And heavily she sighed:
'I think that I have come to shame!'
  And after that she died.

V

The good Queen of England
  Her women came and ran:
'The Little Serving Maid is dead
  From loving of a man!'
Said the good Queen of England
  'That is ill news to hear!
Take her out and shroud her,
  And lay her on a bier.'

VI

They laid her on a bier,
  In the court-yard all;
Some came from Foresting,
  And some came from Hall.
And Great Lords carried her,
  And proud Priests prayed.
And that was the end
  Of the Little Serving Maid.

Auvergnat

There was a man was half a clown
  (It's so my father tells of it).
He saw the church in Clermont town
And laughed to hear the bells of it.

He laughed to hear the bells that ring
In Clermont Church and round of it;
He heard the verger's daughter sing,
And loved her for the sound of it.

The verger's daughter said him nay;
She had the right of choice in it.
He left the town at break of day:
He hadn't had a voice in it.

The road went up, the road went down,
And there the matter ended it.
He broke his heart in Clermont town,
At Pontgibaud they mended it.

Drinking Song

My jolly fat host with your face all a-grin,
Come, open the door to us, let us come in.
A score of stout fellows who think it no sin
If they toast till they're hoarse, and they drink till they spin,
    Hoofed it amain,
    Rain or no rain,
  To crack your old jokes, and your bottle to drain.

Such a warmth in the belly that nectar begets
As soon as his guts with its humour he wets,
The miser his gold, and the student his debts,
And the beggar his rags and his hunger forgets.
    For there's never a wine
    Like this tipple of thine
  From the great hill of Nuits to the River of Rhine.

Outside you may hear the great gusts as they go
By Foy, by Duerne, and the hills of Lerraulx,
But the rain he may rain, and the wind he may blow,
If the Devil's above there's good liquor below.
    So it abound,
    Pass it around,
  Burgundy's Burgundy all the year round.

Drinking Dirge

A thousand years ago I used to dine
   In houses where they gave me such regale
Of dear companionship and comrades fine
   That out I went alone beyond the pale;
And riding, laughed and dared the skies malign
   To show me all the undiscovered tale –
But my philosophy's no more divine,
   I put my pleasure in a pint of ale.

And you, my friends, oh! pleasant friends of mine,
   Who leave me now alone, without avail,
On Californian hills you gave me wine,
   You gave me cider-drink in Longuevaille;
If after many years you come to pine
   For comradeship that is an ancient tale –
You'll find me drinking beer in Dead Man's Chine.
   I put my pleasure in a pint of ale.

In many a briny boat I've tried the brine,
   From many a hidden harbour I've set sail,
Steering towards the sunset where there shine
   The distant amethystine islands pale.
There are no ports beyond the far sea-line,
   Nor any halloa to meet the mariner's hail;
I stand at home and slip the anchor-line.
   I put my pleasure in a pint of ale.

ENVOI

Prince! Is it true that when you go to dine
   You bring your bottle in a freezing pail?
Why then you cannot be a friend of mine.
   I put my pleasure in a pint of ale.

West Sussex Drinking Song

They sell good Beer at Haslemere
    And under Guildford Hill.
At Little Cowfold as I've been told,
    A beggar may drink his fill:
There is a good brew in Amberley too,
    And by the bridge also;
But the swipes they take in at Washington Inn
    Is the very best Beer I know.

CHORUS

    With my here it goes, there it goes,
        All the fun's before us:
    The Tipple's aboard and the night is young,
    The door's ajar and the Barrel is sprung,
    I am singing the best song ever was sung
        And it has a rousing chorus.

If I were what I never can be,
    The master or the squire:
If you gave me the hundred from here to the sea,
    Which is more than I desire:
Then all my crops should be barley and hops,
    And did my harvest fail
I'd sell every rood of mine acres I would
    For a belly-full of good Ale.

CHORUS

    With my here it goes, there it goes,
        All the fun's before us:
    The Tipple's aboard and the night is young,
    The door's ajar and the Barrel is sprung,
    I am singing the best song ever was sung
        And it has a rousing chorus.

A Ballad on Sociological Economics

A while ago it came to pass
   (Merry we carol it all the day),
There sat a man on the top of an ass
   (Heart be happy and carol be gay
     In spite of the price of hay).

And over the down they hoofed it so
   (Happy go lucky has best of fare),
The man up above and the brute below
   (And singing we all forget to care
     A man may laugh if he dare).

Over the stubble and round the crop
   (Life is short and the world is round),
The donkey beneath and the man on the top
   (Oh! let good ale be found, be found,
     Merry good ale and sound).

It happened again as it happened before
   (Tobacco's a boon but ale is bliss),
The moke in the ditch and the man on the floor
   (And that is the moral to this, to this
     Remarkable artifice).

Heretics all, whoever you be,
In Tarbes or Nîmes, or over the sea,
You never shall have good words from me.
  Caritas non conturbat me.

But Catholic men that live upon wine
Are deep in the water, and frank, and fine;
Wherever I travel I find it so,
  Benedicamus Domino.

On childing women that are forlorn,
And men that sweat in nothing but scorn:
That is on all that ever were born,
  Miserere Domine.

To my poor self on my deathbed,
And all my dear companions dead,
Because of the love that I bore them,
  Dona Eis Requiem.

Ha'nacker Mill

Sally is gone that was so kindly
   Sally is gone from Ha'nacker Hill.
And the Briar grows ever since then so blindly
   And ever since then the clapper is still,
   And the sweeps have fallen from Ha'nacker Mill.

Ha'nacker Hill is in Desolation:
   Ruin a-top and a field unploughed.
And Spirits that call on a fallen nation
   Spirits that loved her calling aloud:
   Spirits abroad in a windy cloud.

Spirits that call and no one answers;
   Ha'nacker's down and England's done.
Wind and Thistle for pipe and dancers
   And never a ploughman under the Sun.
   Never a ploughman. Never a one.

Do you remember an Inn,
Miranda?
Do you remember an Inn?
And the tedding and the spreading
Of the straw for a bedding,
And the fleas that tease in the High Pyrenees,
And the wine that tasted of the tar?
And the cheers and the jeers of the young muleteers
(Under the vine of the dark verandah)?
Do you remember an Inn, Miranda,
Do you remember an Inn?
And the cheers and the jeers of the young muleteers
Who hadn't got a penny,
And who weren't paying any,
And the hammer at the doors and the Din?
And the Hip! Hop! Hap!
Of the clap
Of the hands to the twirl and the swirl
Of the girl gone chancing,
Glancing,
Dancing,
Backing and advancing,
Snapping of a clapper to the spin
Out and in –
And the Ting, Tong, Tang of the Guitar!
Do you remember an Inn,
Miranda?
Do you remember an Inn?
Never more;
Miranda,
Never more.
Only the high peaks hoar:
And Aragon a torrent at the door.
No sound
In the walls of the Halls where falls
The tread

Of the feet of the dead to the ground
No sound:
But the boom
Of the far Waterfall like Doom.

Sing to me of the Islands, O daughter of Cohoolin, sing.
      Sing to me of the West:
Sing to me of the girth loosened and the lax harp string
      And of rest.

Beyond the skerries and beyond the outer water
      There lies the land.
Sing to me of the Islands, O daughter of Cohoolin, O High
   King's daughter.
      And of the Overstrand.

I desire to be with Brandan and his companions in the quiet
   places.
      And to drink of their Spring.
Sing to me of the Islands and of the Blessed Faces
      O Daughter of Cohoolin sing!

The Chaunty of the 'Nona'

I

Come list all ye Cullies and Doxies so dear,
You shall hearken to the tale of the Bold Marineer
That took ship out of Holyhead and drove her so hard
Past Bardsey, Pwlheli, Port Madoc, and Fishguard –
Past Bardsey, Pwlheli, Port Madoc, and Fishguard.

II

Then he dropped out of Fishguard on a calm Summer's day,
By St David's and Strumbles and across St Bride's Bay;
Circumnavigating Skomer, that Island, around,
With the heart of a Lion he threaded Jack Sound –
With the heart of a Lion he threaded Jack Sound.

III

But from out the Main Ocean there rolled a great cloud,
So he clawed into Milford Haven by the Fog Blast so loud,
Until he dropped anchor in a deep-wooded bay,
Where all night with Old Sleep and Quiet Sadness he lay –
Where all night with Old Sleep and Quiet Sadness he lay.

IV

Next morning was a Doldrum, and he whistled for a breeze,
Which came from the Nor' Nor' Westward all across the
high seas;
And in passing St Govan's lightship he gave them good
night,
But before it was morning he raised Lundy Light –
Before it was morning he had raised Lundy Light.

V

Then he tossed for twelve hours in that horrible place
Which is known to the Mariner as the Great White Horse
Race,
Till with a slant about three bells, or maybe near four,
He saw white water breaking upon Loud Appledore –
He saw white water breaking upon Loud Appledore.

VI

The Pirates of Appledore, the Wines of Instow;
But her nose is for Bideford with the tide at the flow.
Rattle anchor, batten hatches, and falls all lie curled.
The Long Bridge of Bideford is the end of the World –
The Long Bridge of Bideford is the end of the World.

The Cigadas

Much louder was the Song of the Cigadas
    Upon the Mountain-side, before the day:
The Mountain-side between the two Posadas,
    The two Posadas on Puerto Bay.
    I hear the Sussex Crickets in the hay.
Much louder was the song of the Cigadas.

The Winged Horse

I

It's ten years ago today you turned me out o' doors
To cut my feet on flinty lands and stumble down the shores,
And I thought about the all-in-all, oh more than I can tell!
But I caught a horse to ride upon and I rode him very well,
He had flame behind the eyes of him and wings upon his
    side.
                And I ride, and I ride!

II

I rode him out of Wantage and I rode him up the hill,
And there I saw the Beacon in the morning standing still,
Inkpen and Hackpen and southward and away
High through the middle airs in the strengthening of the
    day,
And there I saw the channel-glint and England in her pride.
                And I ride, and I ride!

III

And once a-top of Lambourne down toward the hill of
    Clere
I saw the Host of Heaven in rank and Michael with his
    spear,
And Turpin out of Gascony and Charlemagne the Lord,
And Roland of the marches with his hand upon his sword
For the time he should have need of it, and forty more
    beside.
                And I ride, and I ride!

IV

For you that took the all-in-all the things you left were
    three.
A loud voice for singing and keen eyes to see,
And a spouting well of joy within that never yet was dried!
                And I ride.

Strephon's Song

When I was not much older
Than Cupid, but bolder,
I asked of his Mother in passing her bower
What it was in their blindness
Men asked of her kindness
And she said it was nought but a delicate flower:
Such a delicate, delicate, delicate flower!

This morning you kissed me,
By noon you dismissed me
As though such great things were the jest of one hour,
And you left me still wondering
If I were not too blundering
To deal with that delicate, delicate flower:
'Tis such a delicate, delicate, delicate flower!

For if that's the complexion
Of Ladies' affection
I must needs be a fool to remain in their power;
But there's that in me burning
Which brings me returning
To beg for the delicate, delicate flower;
To implore for that delicate, delicate flower!

The Fire

I

We rode together all in pride,
They laughing in their riding gowns
We young men laughing at their side,
We charged at will across the downs.

II

We were companions. We were young.
We were immortal – so we said. . . .
For that which in the heart was sung
Could have no commerce with the Dead.

III

Oh! We should live for ever! – Yes!
We were immortal – till there came
Command imposing loneliness
And an extinction of the flame.

IV

And now it's over . . . How it rains!
And now it's over. Though the gale
Gives as of old its gallant hail,
A-driving at the window panes.

V

Lord! How the business disappears!
The golden faces charged with sense
Have broken to accept the years.
And look! what comes to Innocence!

VI

The chosen pictures I retain
Shall perish quickly as shall I.
Only a little while remain
The Downs in their solemnity.

VII

Were they not here, the girls and boys?
I hear them. They are at my call.
The stairs are full of ghostly noise,
But there is no one in the hall.

VIII

The firelight sinks: a reddening shade:
I watch alone beside the fire:
The fire of my good oak is made:
Where is the flower of my desire?

IX

A canker caught it at the root:
A twisted stock: a barren Briar.
It withered. It will bear no fruit.
Where is the flower of my desire?

X

Absolve me, God, that in the land
Which I can nor regard nor know
Nor think about nor understand,
The flower of my desire shall blow.

Dirge

Attend, my gentle brethren of the Weald,
Whom now the frozen field
Does with his caking shell your labour spurn,
And turn your shares and turn
Your cattle homeward to their lazy byres;
Oh! gather round our fires
And point a stave or scald a cleanly churn
The while
With ritual strict and nice observance near,
We weave in decent rhyme
A Threnody for the Departing Year.
And you that since the weary world began,
Subject and dear to man,
Have made a living noise about our homes,
You cows and geese and pigs and sheep and all the crew
Of mice and coneys too
And hares and all that ever lurks and roams
From Harting all the way to Bodiam bend,
Attend!
It is a solemn time,
And we assembled here
Advance in honourable rhyme
With ritual strict and nice observance near
Our Threnody for the Departing Year.

The year shall pass, and yet again the year
Shall on our reeds return
The tufted reeds to hurrying Arun dear. . . .

As I was passing up your landing towns
I heard how in the South a goddess lay.
She ends our little cycle with a pall:
The winter snow shall reverently fall
On our beloved lands,
As on Marana dead a winding sheet
Was laid to hide the smallness of her hands,
And her lips virginal:
Her virginal white feet.

The clouds are high and the skies are wide
  (*It's a weary way to the world's end*).
I hear the wind upon a hillside
  (*Over the hills, away*).

Over the hills and over the sea
  (*It's a weary way to the world's end*).
The woman alone is a-calling me
  (*Over the hills, away*).

Beyond the rim of the rising moon
  (*It's a weary way to the world's end*).
He's back too late who starts too soon
  (*Over the hills, away*).

He's wise, and he laughs who loves to roam
  (*It's a weary way to the world's end*);
He's wise and he cries the when he comes home
  (*Over the hills, away*).

Woman alone, and all alone
  (*It's a weary way to the world's end*).
I'll just be sitting at home, my own,
  The world's a weary way.

A Sussex Drinking Song

On Sussex hills where I was bred,
When lanes in autumn rains are red,
When Arun tumbles in his bed,
  And busy great gusts go by;
When branch is bare in Burton Glen
And Bury Hill is a whitening, then,
I drink strong ale with gentlemen;
  Which nobody can deny, deny,
    Deny, deny, deny, deny,
      Which nobody can deny!

In half-November off I go,
To push my face against the snow,
And watch the winds wherever they blow
  Because my heart is high:
Till I settle me down in Steyning to sing
Of the women I met in my wandering,
And of all that I mean to do in the spring
  Which nobody can deny, deny,
    Deny, deny, deny, deny,
      Which nobody can deny!

Then times be rude and weather be rough,
And ways be foul and fortune tough,
We are of the stout South Country stuff,
That never can have good ale enough,
  And do this chorus cry!
From Crowboro' Top to Ditchling Down,
From Hurstpierpoint to Arundel town,
The girls are plump and the ale is brown:
  Which nobody can deny, deny,
    Deny, deny, deny, deny!
      If he does he tells a lie!

Mrs Rhys

I love to roam from mere caprice
From town to town, from time to time,
Accompanied by Mrs Rhys,
And singing her an elfin rhyme:
    'Star of my wanderings, Mrs Rhys,
    When Mr Rhys shall hear that we
    Were going on like little geese,
    It will annoy him damnably.'

And when because we lack the tin
To pay the sums which they require,
McKenna's minions run us in,
I'll warble in the Black Maria:
    'Light of my dungeon, Mrs Rhys,
    When Mr Rhys shall come to find
    That you are pinched to stretch a piece,
    The thing will prey upon his mind.
    End of existence, Mrs Rhys,
    When Mr Rhys shall hear that you
    Are in the hands of the police
    It will disturb him not a few.'

4
BALLADES

Short Ballade and Postscript on Consols and Boers

I

Gigantic daughter of the West
  (The phrase is Tennysonian), who
From this unconquerable breast
  The vigorous milk of Freedom drew
– We gave it freely – shall the crest
  Of Empire in your keeping true,
Shall England – I forget the rest,
  But Consols are at 82.

II

Now why should anyone invest,
  As even City people do
(His Lordship did among the rest),
  When stocks – but what is that to you?
And then, who ever could have guessed
  About the guns – and horses too! –
Besides, they knew their business best,
  And Consols are at 82.

III

It serves no purpose to protest,
  It isn't manners to halloo
About the way the thing was messed –
  Or vaguely call a man a Jew.
A gentleman who cannot jest
  Remarked that we should muddle through
(The Continent was much impressed),
  And Consols are at 82.

ENVOI

Prince Botha lay at Pilgrim's Rest
  And Myberg in the Great Karroo
(A desert to the south and west),
  And Consols are at 82.

POSTSCRIPT

Permit me – if you do not mind –
　　To add it would be screaming fun
If, after printing this, I find
　　Them after all at 81.

Or 70 or 63,
　　Or 55 or 44,
Or 39 and going free,
　　Or 28 – or even more.

FURTHER ENVOI

No matter – take no more advice
　　From doubtful and intriguing men.
Refuse the stuff at any price,
　　And slowly watch them fall to 10.

Meanwhile I feel a certain zest
　　In writing once again the new
Refrain that all is for the best,
　　And Consols are at 82.

LAST ENVOI

Prince, you and I were barely thirty-three,
　　And now I muse and wonder if it's true,
That you were you and I myself was me,
　　And 3 per cents were really 82!

Ballade of the Unanswered Question

What dwelling hath Sir Harland Pott
  That died of drinking in Bungay?
Nathaniel Goacher who was shot
  Towards the end of Malplaquet?
The only thing that we can say,
  (The only thing that has been said)
About these gentlemen is 'Nay!'
  But where are the unanswering dead?

Lord Bumplepuppy, too, that got
  The knock from Messrs Dawkins' dray?
And Jonas, whom the Cachalot
  Begulphed in Esdraelon Bay?
The Calvinistic John McKay,
  Who argued till his nostrils bled,
And dropped in apoplexy? Nay!
  But where are the unanswering dead?

And Heliodorus too, that hot
  Defender of the Roman sway;
And He, the author of the '*Tot*
  Mercedes dant Victoriae,'
And all the armoured squadrons gay
  That ever glory nourishéd
In all the world's high charges? Nay!
  But where are the unanswering dead?

ENVOI

Prince, have you ever learnt to pray
  Upon your knees beside your bed?
You miserable waxwork? Nay!
  But where are the unanswering dead?

Ballade to Our Lady of Czestochowa

Lady and Queen and Mystery manifold
  And very Regent of the untroubled sky,
Whom in a dream St Hilda did behold
  And heard a woodland music passing by:
  You shall receive me when the clouds are high
With evening and the sheep attain the fold.
This is the faith that I have held and hold,
  And this is that in which I mean to die.

Steep are the seas and savaging and cold
  In broken waters terrible to try;
And vast against the winter night the wold,
  And harbourless for any sail to lie. . . .
  But you shall lead me to the lights, and I
Shall hymn you in a harbour story told.
This is the faith that I have held and hold,
  And this is that in which I mean to die.

Help of the half-defeated, House of gold,
  Shrine of the Sword, and Tower of Ivory;
Splendour apart, supreme and aureoled,
  The Battler's vision and the World's reply.
  You shall restore me, O my last Ally,
To vengeance and the glories of the bold.
This is the faith that I have held and hold,
  And this is that in which I mean to die.

ENVOI

Prince of the degradations, bought and sold,
  These verses, written in your crumbling sty,
Proclaim the faith that I have held and hold
  And publish that in which I mean to die.

Ballade of Hell and of Mrs Roebeck

I'm going out to dine at Gray's
   With Bertie Morden, Charles and Kit,
And Manderly who never pays,
   And Jane who wins in spite of it,
   And Algernon who won't admit
The truth about his curious hair
   And teeth that very nearly fit: –
And Mrs Roebeck will be there.

And then tomorrow someone says
   That someone else has made a hit
In one of Mister Twister's plays.
   And off we go to yawn at it;
   And when it's petered out we quit
For number 20 Taunton Square,
   And smoke, and drink, and dance a bit: –
And Mrs Roebeck will be there.

And so through each declining phase
   Of emptied effort, jaded wit,
And day by day of London days
   Obscurely, more obscurely, lit;
   Until the uncertain shadows flit
Announcing to the shuddering air
   A Darkening, and the end of it: –
And Mrs Roebeck will be there.

ENVOI

Prince, on their iron thrones they sit,
   Impassible to our despair,
The dreadful Guardians of the Pit: –
   And Mrs Roebeck will be there.

Ballade of Unsuccessful Men

The cause of all the poor in '93:
  The cause of all the world at Waterloo:
The shouts of what was terrible and free
  Behind the guns of *Vengeance* and her crew:
The Maid that rode so straightly and so true
  And broke the line to pieces in her pride –
They had to chuck it up: it wouldn't do;
  The Devil didn't like them, and they died.

Caesar and Alexander shall agree
  That right athwart the world their bugles blew:
And all the lads that marched in Lombardy
  Behind the young Napoleon charging through:
All that were easy swordsmen, all that slew
  The Monsters, and that served our God and tried
The temper of this world – they lost the clue.
  The Devil didn't like them, and they died.

You, the strong sons of anger and the sea,
  What darkness on the wings of battle flew?
Then the great dead made answer: 'Also we
  With Nelson found oblivion: Nelson, who
When cheering out of port in spirit grew
  To make one purpose with the wind and tide –
Our nameless hulks are sunk and rotted through:
  The Devil didn't like us and we died.'

ENVOI

Prince, may I venture (since it's only you)
  To speak discreetly of The Crucified?
He was extremely unsuccessful too:
  The Devil didn't like Him, and He died.

John Calvin whose peculiar fad
   It was to call God murderous,
Which further led that feverish cad
   To burn alive the Servetus.
The horrible Bohemian Huss,
   The tedious Wycliffe, where are they?
But where is old Nestorius?
   The wind has blown them all away.

The Kohen out of Novdograd
   Who argued from the Roman Jus
'Privata fasta nihil ad
   Rem nisi sint de sacribus.'
And Hume, who made a dreadful fuss
   About the Resurrection Day
And said it was ridiculous –
   The wind has blown them all away.

Of Smith the gallant Mormon lad
   That took of wives an over-plus:
Johanna Southcott who was mad
   And nasty Nietzsche, who was worse.
Of Tolstoy, the Eccentric Russ,
   Our strong Posterity shall say:
'Lord Jesus! What are these to us?
   The wind has blown them all away!'

ENVOI

Prince, should you meet upon a bus
   A man who makes a great display
Or Dr Haeckel, argue thus: –
   The wind has blown them all away.

Ballade of Good Tidings

The other day the £ fell out of bed
With consequences that are far from clear;
For instance, Eldorado Deeps, instead
Of jumping up, incline to lurch and veer;
And while Commander Turtle thinks it queer
Professor Guff is willing to explain;
But anyhow, the quiet profiteer
Will miss the Riviera and Champagne.

The out o'work will miss his loaf of bread,
The half-at-work will miss his glass of beer,
The City clerk – who might as well be dead –
Will miss the slight advance in his career,
And very many of my friends, I fear,
(Like Algernon, who hasn't got a brain)
A'pacing hollow-eyed on Brighton Pier,
Will miss the Riviera and Champagne.

Ladies and Lords who once on glory fed,
Renaldo, Pharamond and Guinevere,
And Francis, that in glittering armour led
The long defile of Lance and Halberdier;
High Captains of an elder world, give ear –
Caesar and Bonaparte and Charlemagne –
The nobler masters of our modern sphere
Will miss the Riviera and Champagne.

ENVOI

Prince, Oh my Prince, 'Tis heavenly to hear!
Stroke the piano; croon it once again:
'The Rich, the Very Rich, this very year,
Will miss the Riviera and Champagne.'

Ballade of Illegal Ornaments

'... the controversy was ended by His Lordship, who wrote to the Incumbent ordering him to remove from the Church all Illegal Ornaments at once, and especially a Female Figure with a Child.'

When that the Eternal deigned to look
    On us poor folk to make us free,
He chose a Maiden, whom He took
    From Nazareth in Galilee;
    Since when the Islands of the Sea,
The Field, the City, and the Wild
    Proclaim aloud triumphantly
A Female Figure with a Child.

These Mysteries profoundly shook
    The Reverend Doctor Leigh, D.D.,
Who therefore stuck into a Nook
    (Or Niche) of his Incumbency
    An Image filled with majesty
To represent the Undefiled,
    The Universal Mother – She –
A Female Figure with a Child.

His Bishop, having read a book
    Which proved as plain as plain could be
That all the Mutts had been mistook
    Who talked about a Trinity,
    Wrote off at once to Doctor Leigh
In manner very far from mild,
    And said: 'Remove them instantly!
A Female Figure with a Child!'

ENVOI

Prince Jesus, in mine Agony,
    Permit me, broken and defiled,
Through blurred and glazing eyes to see
    A Female Figure with a Child.

Ballade of Genuine Concern

A child at Brighton has been left to drown:
A railway train has jumped the line at Crewe:
I haven't got the change for half a crown:
I can't imagine what on earth to do . . .
Three bisons have stampeded from the Zoo,
A German fleet has anchored in the Clyde.
By God the wretched country's up the flue!
The ice is breaking up on every side.

What! Further news? Rhodesian stocks are down?
England, my England, can the news be true!
Cannot the Duke be got to come to town?
Or will not Mr Hooper pull us through?
And now the Bank is stopping payment too,
The chief cashier has cut his throat and died,
And Scotland Yard has failed to find a clue:
The ice is breaking up on every side.

A raging mob inflamed by Charley Brown
Is tearing up the rails of Waterloo;
They've hanged the Chancellor in wig and gown,
The Speaker, and the Chief Inspector too!
Police! Police! Is this the road to Kew?
I can't keep up: my garter's come untied;
I shall be murdered by the savage crew.
The ice is breaking up on every side.

ENVOI

Prince of the Empire, Prince of Timbuctoo,
Prince eight feet round and nearly four feet wide,
Do try to run a little faster, do.
The ice is breaking up on every side.

Ballade of Gentlemanly Feeling and Railway Strikes

Nothing is more ungentlemanly than
  Exaggeration, causing needless pain;
It's worse than spitting, and it stamps a man
  Deservedly with other men's disdain.
  Weigh human actions carefully. Explain
The worst of them with clarity. Mayhap
  There were two sides to that affair of Cain —
And Judas was a tolerable chap!

This sort of recklessness has laid a ban
  (Most properly!) upon the works of Paine;
And should in decency condemn the clan
  Of mean detractors, like the half-insane
  And filthy Swift, Elijah, and again
The hare-brained Dante, with his snarl and yap —
  No life, however warped, was lived in vain.
And Judas was a tolerable chap.

Benedict Arnold doubtless had a plan
  For profiting his country: it is plain
That nothing but the voice of slander can
  Have poisoned such a man as Charlemagne
  Against the martyred Ganelon in Spain.
We know that Dreyfus fell into a trap —
  Which also may be true of poor Bazaine —
And Judas was a tolerable chap.

ENVOI

Prince, even you are hardly so inane
  As not to understand the sad mishap
Befallen those who run the railway-train —
  And Judas was a tolerable chap.

Ballade of General Misapprehension

The greater part of all the food you eat
   Is chemically poisoned! That is so.
You sicken upon very doubtful meat;
   Your beer is made, I am prepared to show,
   Of SO_3 with too much H_2O.
And that's the reason you have stomach-cold.
   But these are things that people do not know;
They do not know because they are not told.

There is Proclynasis as well as wheat
   And harmless Alum in the baker's dough;
Your salt is made from sweepings of the street,
   The while the peer who sells it you (what ho!)
   Presides by statute over that Bureau
Which legally allows it to be sold:
   But these are things that people do not know;
They do not know because they are not told.

So grin and bear it, Stupid, do not bleat;
   You hungered after progress years ago;
You wanted science and you've got it – neat;
   You certainly desired 'Hygiene' and lo!
   You have it now – and mutter in your woe
Of bitter knowledge dearer bought than gold.
   'These are the things that people do not know;
They do not know because they are not told.'

ENVOI

Prince, have you seen the funny things they grow
   To make your Majesty's Champagne – but hold!
These are the things that people do not know;
   They do not know because they are not told.

5

EPIGRAMS

Epigrams

I
On His Books

When I am dead, I hope it may be said:
'His sins were scarlet, but his books were read.'

II
On Noman, a Guest

Dear Mr Noman, does it ever strike you,
The more we see of you, the less we like you?

III
A Trinity

Of three in One and One in three
My narrow mind would doubting be
Till Beauty, Grace and Kindness met
And all at once were Juliet.

IV
On Torture, a Public Singer

Torture will give a dozen pence or more
To keep a drab from bawling at his door.
The public taste is quite a different thing –
Torture is positively paid to sing.

V
On Paunch, a Parasite

Paunch talks against good liquor to excess,
And then about his raving Patroness;
And then he talks about himself. And then
We turn the conversation on to men.

VI
On Hygiene

Of old when folk lay sick and sorely tried
The doctors gave them physic, and they died.
But here's a happier age: for now we know
Both how to make men sick and keep them so.

VII
On Lady Poltagrue, a Public Peril

The Devil, having nothing else to do,
Went off to tempt My Lady Poltagrue.
My Lady, tempted by a private whim,
To his extreme annoyance, tempted him.

VIII
The Mirror

The mirror held your fair, my Fair,
A fickle moment's space.
You looked into mine eyes, and there
For ever fixed your face.
Keep rather to your looking-glass
Than my more constant eyes;
It told the truth – Alas! my lass,
My faithful memory lies.

IX
The Elm

This is the place where Dorothea smiled.
I did not know the reason, nor did she.
But there she stood, and turned, and smiled at me:
A sudden glory had bewitched the child.
The corn at harvest, and a single tree.
This is the place where Dorothea smiled.

The Telephone

Tonight in million-voicèd London I
Was lonely as the million-pointed sky
Until your single voice. Ah! So the sun
Peoples all heaven, although he be but one.

The Statue

When we are dead, some Hunting-boy will pass
And find a stone half-hidden in tall grass
And grey with age: but having seen that stone
(Which was your image), ride more slowly on.

Epitaph on the Favourite Dog of a Politician

Here lies a Dog: may every Dog that dies
Lie in security – as this Dog lies.

Epitaph on the Politician Himself

Here richly, with ridiculous display,
The Politician's corpse was laid away.
While all of his acquaintance sneered and slanged
I wept: for I had longed to see him hanged.

Another on the Same

This, the last ornament among the peers,
Bribed, bullied, swindled and blackmailed for years:
But Death's what even Politicians fail
To bribe or swindle, bully or blackmail.

XV
On Mundane Acquaintances

Good morning, Algernon: Good morning, Percy.
Good morning, Mrs Roebeck. Christ have mercy!

XVI
On a Rose for Her Bosom

Go, lovely rose, and tell the lovelier fair
That he which loved her most was never there.

XVII
On the Little God

Of all the gods that gave me all their glories
Today there deigns to walk with me but one.
I lead him by the hand and tell him stories.
It is the Queen of Cyprus' little son.

XVIII
On a Prophet

Of old 'twas Samuel sought the Lord: today
The Lord runs after Samuel – so they say.

XIX
On a Dead Hostess

Of this bad world the loveliest and the best
Has smiled and said 'Good Night', and gone to rest.

XX
On a General Election

The accursèd power which stands on Privilege
(And goes with Women, and Champagne and Bridge)
Broke – and Democracy resumed her reign:
(Which goes with Bridge, and Women and Champagne).

XXI
On a Mistaken Mariner

He whistled thrice to pass the Morning Star,
Thinking that near which was so very far.
So I, whenas I meet my Dearest Dear,
Still think that far which is so very near.

XXII
Fatigue

I'm tired of Love: I'm still more tired of Rhyme.
But Money gives me pleasure all the time.

XXIII
On a Sleeping Friend

Lady, when your lovely head
Droops to sink among the Dead,
And the quiet places keep
You that so divinely sleep;
Then the dead shall blessèd be
With a new solemnity,
For such Beauty, so descending,
Pledges them that Death is ending.
Sleep your fill — but when you wake
Dawn shall over Lethe break.

XXIV
On Benicia, who wished Him Well

Benicia wished me well; I wished her well.
And what I wished her more I may not tell.

XXV
The False Heart

I said to Heart, 'How goes it?' Heart replied:
'Right as a Ribstone Pippin!' But it lied.

XXVI
Partly from the Greek

She would be as the stars in your sight
That turn in the endless hollow;
That tremble, and always follow
The quiet wheels of the Night.

XXVII
From the Same

Love's self is sad. Love's lack is sadder still.
But Love unloved, O, that's the greatest ill!

XXVIII
Partly from the Latin

Suns may set and suns may rise,
    Our poor eyes
When their little light is past
    Droop and go to sleep at last.

XXIX
Her Final Role

This man's desire; that other's hopeless end;
A third's capricious tyrant: and my friend.

XXX
On Eyes

Dark eyes adventure bring; the blue serene
Do promise Paradise: and yours are green.

XXXI
On a Hand

Her hand which touched my hand she moved away.
But there it lies, for ever and a day.

XXXII
Obeam Lihens

Insult, despise me; what you can't prevent
Is that my verse shall be your monument.
But, Oh my torment, if you treat me true
I'll cancel every line, for love of you.

XXXIII
On the Ladies of Pixton

Three Graces; and the mother were a Grace,
But for profounder meaning in her face.

XXXIV
The Diamond

This diamond, Juliet, will adorn
Ephemeral beauties yet unborn.
While my strong verse, for ever new,
Shall still adorn immortal you.

XXXV
The Fragment

Towards the evening of her splendid day
Those who are little children now shall say
(Finding this verse), 'Who wrote it, Juliet?'
And Juliet answer gently, 'I forget.'

XXXVI
On a Great House

These are the lawns where Coelia lived and moved;
Was loved, and lovely was: but never loved.

XXXVII
On Vital Statistics

'*Ill* fares the land to hast'ning *ills* a prey[1]
Where wealth accumulates and men decay.'
But how much more unfortunate are those
Where wealth declines and population grows!

1. This line is execrable; and I note it.
   I quote it as the faulty poet wrote it.

XXXVIII
Criterion

When you are mixed with many I descry
A single light, and judge the rest thereby.
But when you are alone with me, why then,
I quite forget all women and all men.

XXXIX
The Face

A face Sir Joshua might have painted? Yea:
Sir Joshua painted anything for pay . . .
And after all you're painted every day.

XL
On Two Ministers of State

Lump says that Caliban's of gutter breed,
And Caliban says Lump's a fool indeed,
And Caliban, and Lump and I are all agreed.

XLI
On Chelsea

I am assured by Dauber's wife
That Dauber's always true to life.
I think his wife would far prefer
That Dauber should be true to her.

XLII
The Pacifist

Pale Ebenezer thought it wrong to fight,
But Roaring Bill (who killed him) thought it right.

XLIII
On another Politician

The politician, dead and turned to clay,
Will make a clout to keep the wind away.
I am not fond of draughts, and yet I doubt
If I could get myself to touch that clout.

XLIV
On yet Another

Fame to her darling Shifter glory gives;
And Shifter is immortal, while he lives.

XLV
On a Puritan

He served his God so faithfully and well
That now he sees him face to face, in hell.

XLVI
On the little God

The love of God which leads to realms above
Is contre-carréd by the God of Love.

XLVII
On a Sundial

In soft deluding lies let fools delight.
A Shadow marks our days; which end in Night.

XLVIII
On the Same

How slow the Shadow creeps: but when 'tis past
How fast the Shadows fall. How fast! How fast!

XLIX
On the Same

Loss and Possession, Death and Life are one.
There falls no shadow where there shines no sun.

L
On the Same

Stealthy the silent hours advance, and still;
And each may wound you, and the last shall kill.

LI
On the Same
Here in a lonely glade, forgotten, I
Mark the tremendous process of the sky.
So does your inmost soul, forgotten, mark
The Dawn, the Noon, the coming of the Dark.

LII
On the Same

I that still point to one enduring star
Abandoned am, as all the Constant are.

LIII
On the Same

Save on the rare occasions when the Sun
Is shining, I am only here for fun.

LIV
On the Same

I am a sundial, and I make a botch
Of what is done far better by a watch.

LV
On the Same

I am a sundial, turned the wrong way round.
I cost my foolish mistress fifty pound.

LVI
On the Same

Creep, shadow, creep: my ageing hours tell;
I cannot stop you, so you may as well.

LVII
Rose

Rose, little Rose, the youngest of the Roses,
My little Rose whom I may never see,
When you shall come to where the heart reposes
Cut me a Rose and send it down to me.

When you shall come into the High Rose-Gardens,
Where Roses bend upon Our Lady's Tree,
The place of Plenitudes, the place of Pardons,
Cut me a Rose and send it down to me.

LVIII
Triolet

The young, the lovely and the wise,
    Their face is set toward their going.
They pass me with indifferent eyes,
The young, the lovely and the wise,
And fill me with a long surmise
Upon my losing and my owing . . .
The young, the lovely and the wise,
    Their face is set toward their going.

LIX
Habitations

Kings live in Palaces, and Pigs in sties,
And youth in Expectation. Youth is wise.

LX
On a Great Name

I heard today Godolphin say
He never gave himself away.
Come, come Godolphin, scion of kings,
Be generous in little things.

LXI

Is there any reward?
   I'm beginning to doubt it.
I am broken and bored,
   Is there any reward?
Reassure me, Good Lord,
   And inform me about it,
Is there any reward?
   I'm beginning to doubt it.

LXII

In Barbary when I was young
   A woman singing through the night,
The scented lemon trees among
   In Barbary when I was young.

The song that in the night was sung,
   By Lailah the Rahabite.
In Barbary when I was young,
   A woman singing through the night.

LXIII
Talking of Bad Verse

William, you vary greatly in your verse:
Some's none too good, but all the rest is worse.

LXIV
An Example of the Same

Wine exercises a peculiar charm;
But, taken in excess, does grievous harm.

LXV
Juliet

How did the party go in Portman Square?
I cannot tell you; Juliet was not there.
And how did Lady Gaster's party go?
Juliet was next me and I do not know.

LXVI
From the Latin (but not so pagan)

Blessed is he that has come to the heart of the world and is
  humble.
He shall stand alone; and beneath
His feet are implacable fate, and panic at night, and the
  strumble
Of the hungry river of death.

LXVII
Epitaph

Here William lies, in truth; before he died
For forty mortal years in truth he lied.

LXVIII
A Modest Politician

Godolphin says he does not wish to swell
The Roll of Fame; and it is just as well.

LXIX
On his Home, King's Land

Stand thou forever among human Houses,
House of the Resurrection, House of Birth;
House of the rooted hearts and long carouses,
Stand, and be famous over all the Earth.

LXX
Epitaph upon Himself

Lauda tu Ilarion audacem et splendidum
Who was always beginning things and never ended 'em.

LXXI

Discovery

Life is a long discovery, isn't it?
You only get your wisdom bit by bit.
If you have luck you find in early youth
How dangerous it is to tell the Truth;
And next you learn how dignity and peace
Are the ripe fruits of patient avarice.
You find that middle life goes racing past.
You find despair: and, at the very last,
You find as you are giving up the ghost
That those who loved you best despised you most.

6

LONGER POEMS

The Ballad of Val-ès-Dunes

THE VICTORY OF WILLIAM THE CONQUEROR
IN HIS YOUTH OVER THE REBELS AT
VAL-ÈS-DUNES IN THE YEAR 1047

This piece of verse is grossly unhistorical. Val-ès-Dunès is not on the sea but inland. No Norman blazoned a shield or a church window in the middle eleventh century, still less would he frame one in silver, and I doubt gilt spurs. It was not the young Bastard of Falaise, but the men of the King in Paris that really won the battle. There was nothing Scandinavian left in Normandy, and whatever there had been five generations before was slight. The Cotentin had no more Scandinavian blood than the rest. There is no such place as Longuevaile. There is a Hauteville, but it has no bay and had nothing to do with the Harcourts, and the Harcourts were not of Blood Royal – and so forth.

I

The men that lived in Longuevaile
　　Came out to fight by bands.
They jangled all in welded mail,
Their shields were rimmed of silver pale
And blazoned like a church-vitrail:
　　Their swords were in their hands.
But the harsh raven of the Old Gods
　　Was on the rank sea-sands.

　　　．　　．　　．　　．　　．

There rose a wind on heath and den:
　　The sky went racing grey.
The Bastard and his wall of men
　　Were a charger's course away.

II

The Old Gods of the Northern Hall
　　Are in their narrow room.
Their thrones are flanked of spearmen tall,
The three that have them in their thrall,
Sit silently before them all,
　　They weave upon their loom;
And round about them as they weave
　　The Scalds sing doom.

III

The Bastard out of Normandy
  Was angry for his wrong.
His eyes were virginal to see,
For nothing in his heart had he
But a hunger for his great degree;
  And his back was broad and strong
As are the oxen of the field,
  That pull the ploughs along.

IV

He saw that column of cavalry wheel,
  Split outward, and deploy.
He heard, he heard the Oliphant peal.
He crooked an angry knee to feel
The scabbard against his gilded heel.
  He had great joy:
And he stood upright in the stirrup steel
  Because he was a boy.

   .   .   .   .   .

  We faced their ordering, all the force,
    And there was little sound;
  But Haribert-Le-Marshall's horse
    Pawed heavily the ground.

V

As the broad ships out of Barbary
  Come driving from the large,
With yards a-bend and courses free,
And tumbling down their decks a-lee
The hurrahing of the exultant sea,
  So drave they to the charge.
But the harsh raven of the Old Gods
  Was on the rank sea-marge.

VI

The Old Gods of the Northern Hall
   Are crownéd for the tomb.
Their biers are flanked of torches tall,
And through the flames that leap and fall.
There comes a droning and a call
   To the night's womb,
As the tide beneath a castle wall
   Goes drumming through the gloom.

VII

They tonsured me but Easter year,
   I swore to Christ and Rome.
My name is not mine older name . . .
But ah! to see them as they came,
With thundering and with points aflame,
   I smelt foam.
And my heart was like a wandering man's,
Who piles his boat on Moorna sands
   And serves a slave in alien lands,
And then beneath a harper's hands
   Hears suddenly of home.

.   .   .   .   .

For their cavalry came in a curling leaf,
   They shouted as they drave,
And the Bastard's line was like a reef
   But theirs was like a wave.

VIII

As the broad ships out of Barbary
   Strike rock.
And the stem shatters, and the sail flaps;
Streaming seaward; and the taut shroud snaps,
And the block
   Clatters to the deck of the wreck.
So did the men of Longuevaile
   Take the shock.

IX

Our long line quivered but it did not break,
  It countered and was strong.
The first bolt went through the wind with a wail,
And another and a-many with a thudding on the mail;
Pattered all the arrows in an April hail;
  Whistled the ball and thong:
And I, the priest, with that began
  The singing of my song.

X

Press inward, inward, Normandy;
  Press inward, Cleres and Vaux;
Press inward, Mons and Valéry;
  Press inward, Yvetot.
Stand hard the men of the Beechen Ford
(Oh! William of Falaise, my lord!)
Battle is a net and a struggle in a cord.
  Battle is a wrestler's throw.
The middle holding as the wings made good,
The far wings closing as the centre stood.
Battle is a mist and battle is a wood,
  And battle is won so.

XI

The fishermen fish in the River of Seine,
  They haul the long nets in.
They haul them in and they haul again,
(The fishermen fish in the River of Seine)
They haul them in and they haul again,
  A million glittering fin:
With the hauling in of our straining ends
  That Victory did begin.

XII

The tall son of the Seven Winds
   Galloped hot-foot from the Hither Hithe.
So strongly went he down the press,
Almost he did that day redress
With his holping and his hardiness,
   For his sword was like a scythe
In Arques when the grass is high,
And all the swathes in order lie,
And there's the bailiff standing by —
   A-gathering of the tithe.

XIII

And now, go forward, Normandy,
   Go forward all in one.
The press was caught and trampled and it broke
From the sword and its swinger and the axe's stroke,
Pouring through the gap in a whirl of smoke
   As a blinded herd will run.
And so fled many and a very few
With mounts all spent would staggering pursue,
But the race fell scattered as the evening grew:
   The battle was over and done.

   •   •   •   •   •

Like Birds against the reddening day
*   They dwindled one by one,*
And I heard a trumpet far away
*   At the setting of the sun.*

   •   •   •   •   •

XIV

The stars were in the Eternal Sky,
   It was calm in Massared;
Richard, Abbot of Leclair, and I
And a Picard Priest that held on high
   A Torch above his head;
We stumbled through the darkening land
Assoiling with anointed hand
   The dying and the dead.

How many in the tufted grass,
   How many dead there lay.
For there was found the Fortenbras
And young Garain of Hault, alas!
And the Wardens of the Breton pass
   Who were lords of his array,
And Hugh that trusted in his glass
   But came not home the day.

I saw the miller of Martindall,
   I saw that archer die.
The blunt quarrel caught him at the low white wall,
And he tossed up his arrow to the Lord God of all,
But long before the first could fall
   His soul was in the sky.

The last of all the lords that sprang
   From Harcourt of the Crown,
He parried with the shield and the silver rang,
But the axe fell heavy on the helm with a clang
And the girths parted and the saddle swang,
   And he went down:
   He never more sang winter songs
   In his high town.

In his high town that Faëry is,
   And stands on Harcourt bay,
The fisher surging through the night
Takes bearing by that castle height,
And moors him harboured in the bight,
   And watches for the day.
But with the broadening of the light,
   It vanishes away.

XIX

In his high town that Faëry is,
   And stands on Harcourt Lea.
To summon him up his arrier-ban,
His writ beyond the mountains ran;
My father was his serving man,
   Although the farm was free.
Before the angry wars began
   He was a friend to me.

XX

The night before the boy was born
   There came a Priest who said
That he had seen red Aldeborn,
The star of hate in Taurus' horn,
Which glared above a field of corn,
   And covered him with dread.
I wish to God I had not held
   The cloth in which he bled.

     .   .   .   .   .

XXI

The Horse from Cleres and Valéry,
   The foot from Yvetot,
And all the men of the Harbour Towns
   That live by fall and flow.
And all the men of the Beechen Ford
– Oh! William of Falaise, my lord! –
And all the sails in Michael's ward,
And all the shields of Caux,
   Shall follow you out across the world,
   With sword and lance and bow,
To Beachy and to Pevensey Bar,
   To Chester through the snow,
With sack and pack and camping tent,
   A-grumbling as they go:
My lord is William of Falaise.
   Haro!

Heroic Poem in Praise of Wine

TO DUFF COOPER

To exalt, enthrone, establish and defend,
To welcome home mankind's mysterious friend:
Wine, true begetter of all arts that be;
Wine, privilege of the completely free;
Wine the recorder; wine the sagely strong;
Wine, bright avenger of sly-dealing wrong,
Awake, Ausonian Muse, and sing the vineyard song!

Sing how the Charioteer from Asia came,
And on his front the little dancing flame
Which marked the God-head. Sing the Panther-team,
The gilded Thyrsus twirling, and the gleam
Of cymbals through the darkness. Sing the drums.
He comes: the young renewer of Hellas comes!
The Seas await him. Those Aegean Seas
Roll from the dawning, ponderous, ill at ease
In lifts of lead, whose cresting hardly breaks
To ghostly foam, when suddenly there awakes
A mountain glory inland. All the skies
Are luminous; and amid the sea bird cries
The mariner hears a morning breeze arise.
Then goes the Pageant forward. The sea-way
Silvers the feet of that august array
Trailing above the waters, through the airs;
And as they pass a wind before them bears
The quickening word, the influence magical.
The Islands have received it, marble-tall;
The long shores of the mainland. Something fills
The warm Euboean combes, the sacred hills
Of Aulis and of Argos. Still they move
Touching the City walls, the Temple grove,
Till, far upon the horizon-glint, a gleam
Of light, of trembling light, revealed they seem
Turned to a cloud, but to a cloud that shines,
And everywhere as they pass, the Vines! The Vines!

The Vines, the conquering Vines! And the Vine breathes
Her savour through the upland, empty heaths
Of treeless wastes; the Vines have come to where
The dark Pelasgian steep defends the lair
Of the wolf's hiding; to the empty fields
By Aufidus, the dry campaign that yields
No harvest for the husbandman, but now
Shall bear a nobler foison than the plough;
To where, festooned along the tall elm trees,
Tendrils are mirrored in Tyrrhenian seas;
To where the South awaits them; even to where
Stark, African, informed of burning air,
Upturned to Heaven the broad Hipponian plain
Extends luxurious and invites the main.
Guelma's a mother: barren Thapsa breeds;
And northward in the valleys, next the meads
That sleep by misty river banks, the Vines
Have struck to spread below the solemn pines.
The Vines are on the roof-trees. All the Shrines
And Homes of men are consecrate with Vines.

And now the task of that triumphant day
Has reached to victory. In the reddening ray
With all his train, from hard Iberian lands
Fulfilled, apparent, that Creator stands
Halted on Atlas. Far beneath him, far,
The strength of Ocean darkening and the star
Beyond all shores. There is a silence made.
It glorifies: and the gigantic shade
Of Hercules adores him from the West.

Dead Lucre: burnt Ambition: Wine is best.

But what are these that from the outer murk
Of dense mephitic vapours creeping lurk
To breathe foul airs from that corrupted well
Which oozes slime along the floor of Hell?
   These are the stricken palsied brood of sin
   In whose vile veins, poor, poisonous and thin,

Decoctions of embittered hatreds crawl:
These are the Water-Drinkers, cursed all!
On what gin-sodden Hags, what flaccid sires
Bred these White Slugs from what exhaust desires?
In what close prison's horror were their wiles
Watched by what tyrant power with evil smiles?
Or in what caverns, blocked from grace and air
Received they, then, the mandates of despair?
What! Must our race, our tragic race, that roam
All exiled from our first, and final, home:
That in one moment of temptation lost
Our heritage, and now wander, hunger-tost
Beyond the Gates (still speaking with our eyes
For ever of remembered Paradise),
Must we with every gift accepted, still,
With every joy, receive attendant ill?
Must some lewd evil follow all our good
And muttering dog our brief beatitude?

A primal doom, inexorable, wise,
Permitted, ordered, even these to rise.
Even in the shadow of so bright a Lord
Must swarm and propagate the filthy horde
Debased, accursed I say, abhorrent and abhorred.
Accursed and curse-bestowing. For whosoe'er
Shall suffer their contagion, everywhere
Falls from the estate of man and finds his end
To the mere beverage of the beast condemned.

For such as these in vain the Rhine has rolled
Imperial centuries by hills of gold;
For such as these the flashing Rhône shall rage
In vain its lightning through the Hermitage,
Or level-browed divine Touraine receive
The tribute of her vintages at eve
For such as these Burgundian heats in vain
Swell the rich slope or load the empurpled plain.
Bootless for such as these the mighty task
Of bottling God the Father in a flask

And leading all Creation down distilled
To one small ardent sphere immensely filled.
With memories empty, with experience null,
With vapid eye-balls meaningless and dull
They pass unblest through the unfruitful light;
And when we open the bronze doors of Night,
When we in high carousal, we, reclined,
Spur up to Heaven the still ascending mind,
Pass with the all inspiring, to and fro,
The torch of genius and the Muse's glow,
They, lifeless, stare at vacancy alone
Or plan mean traffic, or repeat their moan.
We, when repose demands us, welcomed are
In young white arms, like our great Exemplar
Who, wearied with creation, takes his rest
And sinks to sleep on Ariadne's breast.
They through the darkness into darkness press
Despised, abandoned and companionless.

And when the course of either's sleep has run
We leap to life like heralds of the sun;
We from the couch in roseate mornings gay
Salute as equals the exultant day
While they, the unworthy, unrewarded, they
The dank despisers of the Vine, arise
To watch grey dawns and mourn indifferent skies.

Forget them! Form the Dionysian ring
And pulse the ground, and Io, Io, sing.

Father Lenaean, to whom our strength belongs,
Our loves, our wars, our laughter and our songs,
Remember our inheritance, who praise
Your glory in these last unhappy days
When beauty sickens and a muddied robe
Of baseness fouls the universal globe.
Though all the Gods indignant and their train
Abandon ruined man, do thou remain!
By thee the vesture of our life was made,
The Embattled Gate, the lordly Colonnade,

The woven fabric's gracious hues, the sound
Of trumpets, and the quivering fountain-round,
And, indestructible, the Arch, and, high,
The Shaft of Stone that stands against the sky,
And, last, the guardian-genius of them, Rhyme,
Come from beyond the world to conquer time:
All these are thine, Lenaean.

By thee do seers the inward light discern;
By thee the statue lives, the Gods return;
By thee the thunder and the falling foam
Of loud Acquoria's torrent call to Rome;
Alba rejoices in a thousand springs,
Gensano laughs, and Orvieto sings . . .
But, Ah! With Orvieto, with that name
Of dark, Etrurian, subterranean flame
The years dissolve. I am standing in that hour
Of majesty Septembral, and the power
Which swells the clusters when the nights are still
With autumn stars on Orvieto hill.

Had these been mine, Ausonian Muse, to know
The large contented oxen heaving slow;
To count my sheaves at harvest; so to spend
Perfected days in peace until the end;
With every evening's dust of gold to hear
The bells upon the pasture height, the clear
Full horn of herdsmen gathering in the kine
To ancient byres in hamlets Apennine,
And crown abundant age with generous ease:
Had these, Ausonian Muse, had these, had these . . .
But since I would not, since I could not stay,
Let me remember even in this my day
How, when the ephemeral vision's lure is past
All, all, must face their Passion at the last.
Was there not one that did to Heaven complain
How, driving through the midnight and the rain,
He struck, the Atlantic seethe and surge before,
Wrecked in the North along a lonely shore

To make the lights of home and hear his name no more?
Was there not one that from a desperate field
Rode with no guerdon but a rifted shield;
A name disherited; a broken sword;
Wounds unrenowned; battle beneath no Lord;
Strong blows, but on the void, and toil without reward?

When from the waste of such long labour done
I too must leave the grape-ennobling sun
And like the vineyard worker take my way
Down the long shadows of declining day,
Bend on the sombre plain my clouded sight
And leave the mountain to the advancing night,
Come to the term of all that was mine own
With nothingness before me, and alone;
Then to what hope of answer shall I turn?
Comrade-Commander whom I dared not earn,
What said You then to trembling friends and few?
'A moment, and I drink it with you new:
But in my Father's Kingdom.' So, my Friend,
Let not Your cup desert me in the end.
But when the hour of mine adventure's near,
Just and benignant, let my youth appear
Bearing a Chalice, open, golden, wide,
With benediction graven on its side.
So touch my dying lip: so bridge that deep:
So pledge my waking from the gift of sleep,
And, sacramental, raise me the Divine:
Strong brother in God and last companion, Wine.

Index of First Lines

183

184

186

*Some books in various
Penguin Series are described in
the remaining pages*

GERARD MANLEY HOPKINS

A SELECTION OF HIS POEMS AND PROSE

BY W. H. GARDNER

D 15

Since the posthumous works of Gerard Manley Hopkins first displayed their 'plumage of far wonder and heavenward flight' in the collection of 1918, which was edited by Robert Bridges, they have gone into a Third Edition and run through thirteen impressions. His prose has hitherto been published only in expensive volumes, two of which are now temporarily out of print. The selection in the Penguin Poets includes the forty-eight mature poems and thirteen of the best 'unfinished poems and fragments'. These are preceded by two early pieces and also by the 'Author's Preface', in which Hopkins explains his highly original prosody. Notes have been added to help the general reader to understand the poet's thought and to elucidate further his Sprung, Counterpointed, and 'outriding' rhythms.

The prose passages have been taken mainly from the journals and letters, but they include also extracts from a Platonic dialogue, a sermon, and a commentary. They have been chosen with the purpose of filling in the portrait of this Victorian Jesuit, whose personality and vision are as significant as his brilliant poetic technique. The editor's critical and biographical Introduction stresses the importance of the poet's theory of 'inscape' and 'instress' and aims generally at giving a certain unity to the whole selection.

THE PENGUIN SHAW